To Dot -

 a delightful friend
and a true artist.
Thanks for being
just you!

 Hope you will
enjoy nature's
treasures as much
as I

 fondly,

 Mary E. Thompson

June 1972

The Driftwood Book

Driftwood is an effective element in a composition with strelitzia flowers, aspidistra leaves, and a primitive African head.

The Driftwood Book

BY

MARY E. THOMPSON

WITH PHOTOGRAPHS BY LEONID SKVIRSKY

SECOND EDITION

D. VAN NOSTRAND COMPANY, INC.

PRINCETON, NEW JERSEY

TORONTO   LONDON

Van Nostrand Regional Offices: *New York, Chicago, San Francisco*

D. Van Nostrand Company, Ltd., *London*

D. Van Nostrand Company (Canada), Ltd., *Toronto*

Library of Congress Catalog Card No. 60-9037

Second Edition Published January 1966
Reprinted May 1967

PRINTED IN THE UNITED STATES OF AMERICA

TO MY HUSBAND
whose self-sacrifice
made this book possible

Editor's Foreword: "To Make Visible"

"To make visible the invisible," that we are told is the principle function of the artist. Ten years ago to how many flower arrangers was driftwood "visible"? Not many, I imagine, since the artists among them had hardly begun to discover the beauty of wood cast up by sea and lake, discarded by forest trees, or strewn on the desert where sun and wind bleached each piece to a wonderful silver-gray. But like the beauty of natural rocks and stones discovered centuries ago by the Japanese and to-day valued in their gardens or homes as precious *objets d'art,* the beauty of wood in its natural condition has now been made visible to many floral artists; for our awareness we are assuredly grateful to Mary E. Thompson, one of the first to see this marvelous potential. Her designs with driftwood are, indeed, unique and her compositions featuring it wonderfully versatile.

No other arranger to my knowledge has handled driftwood with such respect for its inherent strength, its sculptural shapes, its varied patina and coloring. Mrs. Thompson knows how to bring out to the fullest the textural differences in the many kinds of bark with their amazing striations and how to develop lovely and arresting designs with flowers, foliages, fruits and figures.

The pictures in this book speak eloquently of her talent for arranging and of her "way," as the Japanese say it, with flowers and driftwood. The photographs attest also to the great skill of the photographer, Leonid Skvirsky. His sensitive use of light has emphasized every nuance of his subject.

These pictures, selected from a much greater number, will speak to all collectors of decorative wood. The traditionalist will take pleasure in designs of a type that has long been considered pleasing. The modernist will dwell with excitement upon the thirty-two contemporary designs presented in this extended 1966 version of the definitive text.

My favorites among these 160 expressive compositions are now too numerous to mention. I can only say that Mrs. Thompson was the first to make vividly visible to me the manifold beauties of driftwood.

HELEN VAN PELT WILSON

Contents

Acknowledgments

I wish to express my appreciation to Mr. Leonid Skvirsky for his cooperation during the photography; to the many friends who were so considerate while the book was in progress; to those who graciously shared their gardens with me, and to others with whom I shared the joys of "driftwood hunting." Special thanks go to many who gave me encouragement when it was most needed. Each friend has had a part in this book.

MARY E. THOMPSON

Introduction: Driftwood -- Living Beauty

Living beauty, these are the words that appropriately describe driftwood. It *is* living beauty! In its shape, rhythm, grain, it retains the rugged, enduring life force that everywhere captivates the flower arranger and the lover of art. Instead of running the course of a fad, as many expected when driftwood first appeared in arrangements, its popularity has increased with the years. Not only is it accepted as a vital element in compositions for homes, offices and flower shows, but being beautiful in itself, it is also sought by art collectors and enjoyed as a piece of fine sculpture. Driftwood is indeed all things to all people, and somewhere there is a piece of driftwood to delight even the most blasé.

This decorative wood is the perfect accompaniment for natural materials. Being both beautiful and practical, it has played an important part in the evaluation of flower arrangement. As we consider designs from all over the country, we realize that there has been a vast change in designing since the first garden club in America was organized in the little town of Athens, Georgia, some seventy years ago. A new look has evolved as the rich traditions of the past have been fused with the present to produce a highly creative period in flower arrangement.

Because of its boldness of line and form, driftwood is now playing a leading rôle, for it can be combined effectively with the many new materials accepted for use in designing. It is selected by arrangers both for its naturalistic appeal and for its use in modern and abstract styles.

I hope you discover in the text and photographs of this book the marvelous versatility of driftwood. Like fingerprints, no two pieces are alike. And every piece has many potential uses. Driftwood can be found almost everywhere. In fact, there is hardly a place where you cannot find weatherbeaten, wind-blown, sun-bleached and insect-riddled pieces of decorative wood—roots as well as branches. When you discover a gnarled, contorted branch you have the challenge of deciding whether to leave it as it is or to improve its shape and appearance by pruning, polishing and bleaching.

All of the mechanics of dealing with driftwood— where to find and how to prepare it—are considered in Part One of this book. The art of creating effective arrangements begins with the illustrations in Part Two. In Part Three newer trends are discussed and illustrated. These designs suggest only a few of the fascinating possibilities. Interpretations of a design are simply my private impressions; each design may impress you differently.

Driftwood is invariably an eye-catcher, an unfailing topic of conversation. Mounted on a wall, used in a planter, made into a base for a lamp or table, lending strength, rhythm and distinction to a flower arrangement, employed in abstract designing, or alone as an *objet d'art*—driftwood has magic. You too, will fall under its spell.

Part I
THE MECHANICS

1. Where to Find Driftwood

In conversations and at lecture-demonstrations I am invariably asked: "Where do you find all your lovely driftwood?" The question is so inevitable that I have learned to discuss that problem first. And it is a problem nowadays—a problem that can only become more difficult as the number of driftwood-hunters increases.

Beaches

The popular name for these pieces of decorative wood, driftwood, indicates the most common place to look for them—ocean beaches. But that's just the trouble: Everyone has the same idea. Beaches are ideal places to collect wood that has drifted in from the ocean, provided you get there before someone else has garnered it all. If you live near a beach, the chances are that a few thousand other people do, too. And some of them are sure to be driftwood enthusiasts. You almost have to be on the strand at the crack of dawn, especially if the beach gets daily attention from a municipal clean-up crew. An alternative is to tour the coastline till you find an out-of-

3

the-way yet reasonably accessible beach. (You may need ropes and an alpenstock to reach it, but get there!)

The day after a storm at sea is an excellent time to comb the beaches for wonderful treasures. At such a time your early rising is most likely to be richly rewarded. Wood swept in from the sea possesses unique qualities and textures. The lashing, abrasive force of the water begins the process as the wood is washed ashore. Then constant lapping of gentle waves plus the effect of sand, sun and wind, and even the attacks of parasites, help to create a thing of beauty that is a joy to own.

Lake Shores

If the shore of an ocean (or gulf, sound or bay) is not convenient to you, do not despair, for then you surely live near some inland waterway. Perhaps you are close to one of the many lakes or ponds—either natural or man-made—that beautify our country. From Huron and Superior to the tiniest bodies of water, a lake is likely to be an excellent hunting ground. Unlike the wood found on the seacoast, which is usually large and heavy, driftwood found around lakes is generally somewhat smaller and much lighter in weight, also of more graceful form.

Late fall or winter, when water levels are low, is the

4

time to go driftwood-hunting around the lakes. In anticipation of heavy winter rains, many artificial lakes are
drained to some extent in the fall. As the water recedes,
pieces of wood are left stranded within easy reach of the
searcher. Certainly before the water climbs back to its
usual spring level, you should plan a driftwood excursion.

While on such an excursion, be careful not to overlook
the curved roots still attached to huge root sections which
untutored searchers usually pass by. These can be broken
or sawed off in various lengths and forms. Even the
stubby, chunky bases of small tree roots have possibilities. Combined with rhythmically shaped limbs or
branches, they can be quite striking, as you can see in
Plates 5, 6 and 7. Train yourself to look for and recognize
the value of such pieces. Then put your ingenuity to work.
You may be surprised by the many attractive combinations you can achieve.

Plates 1, 2, 3 and 4. The eleven pieces of driftwood in these four
plates might be called "A Pageant of Natural Forms." They are
a small but typical sample of the fabulous variety of decorative
wood pieces that Nature creates. Driftwood can be used to great
advantage with flowers, foliage and fruit; but, as shown, it often
is sufficiently bizarre to produce a startling effect by itself.

5

Plate 1

Plate 2

Plate 3

Plate 4

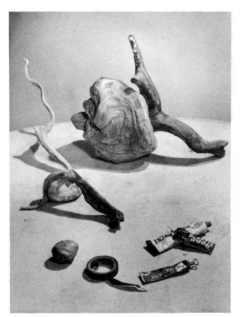

Plates 5 and 6. A bit of glue and imagination can convert two rather pedestrian pieces into a whole that is considerably more than twice as interesting as either of its parts. These two before-and-after photographs of a chunky root section and a single branch illustrate the point. Note that the glued area has been bound in floral tape to hold the union firmly until dry.

Plate 7. A practiced eye can visualize a form of great beauty from the joining of this root remnant and branch. To check your opinion of this against the finished product see Plate 84.

Coves

Take it from an old driftwood prospector, don't over-look the coves up and down the lake. If you aren't satis-fied with the pieces you find as you walk along the main lake shores, get yourself a boat and explore the coves. This is often the only way to reach them, and your efforts may be richly rewarded. Wood that drifts into these coves is held in by the lapping waves. The accumulation in-creases until one day a storm or a driftwood-hunter pays a call and—poof—the cove is empty.

Around Dams

Dams are built for electric power, irrigation or flood-control. And they create artificial lakes. These dams often are tremendous structures but, of more immediate con-cern, they serve as collection points for tree roots, limbs and old pieces of board that have found their way into water. These come drifting down from all parts of the lake. If boating near the dam is permissible, you may be able to scoop some good items right out of the water. If the water level of an artificial lake drops or is intention-ally lowered, the exposed land should yield some choice pieces. One of my favorite, and most remarkable, pieces was discovered while on one of these low-water treasure

hunts. I have used it in Plate 8. It is a wonderfully textured old piece of board, probably in the water for years
before its exposure. The sun completed the treatment by
giving it a lovely gray patina.

Mountain Forests and Streams

If you are vacationing in the mountains, or simply on
a one-day excursion, set aside some time for a driftwood
hunt. Storms and fires raging through heavily timbered
regions of the mountains leave all kinds of debris in
their wake. Unusual wood formations are produced
when tender branches are unmercifully torn and twisted.
Other trees are uprooted to lie and rot on the ground.
After long exposure the bark of these decaying logs
loosens and it is easily removed in sections. Some of these
pieces will serve as trays or can be used as versatile bases
(see Plate 60). The wood itself acquires a mellow,
weathered look, softer than the effect wrought by waves
or other influences.

A stroll along a mountain stream where mountain
laurel and rhododendron abound is likely to prove fruit-
ful if you are a determined searcher for the unusual.
These broadleaved evergreens often have peculiar quirks
of growth. The discovery of an uprooted specimen with
wondrous gnarls, loops and twists will repay you abund-

11

antly for your effort. Since you will probably want only parts of the plant, and since these limbs and roots are not easily broken, it is wise to take along a lightweight saw on this type of outing.

Here let me inject a passing thought that applies to all of these situations. Children are indefatigable collectors of anything and everything. You'll have no trouble enlisting their aid. Of course you may get only one good piece out of a hundred eagerly submitted, but just remember to be diplomatic about the ninety-nine rejects and you won't lose your helpers.'

From the Desert

The desert areas of our country may also yield interesting "ghostwood." Some people think of the desert as a dry, barren place without a vestige of life, unblessed by rain and plagued by sandstorms. That of course is far from a true picture, even of Death Valley. In addition to

---

Plate 8. Every piece of driftwood has its best position, but often it needs a "mechanical aid" to support it in that position. (See Chapter 3.) With a small, similarly textured piece of wood screwed to the bottom, this deeply serrated slab of driftwood can stand firmly upright. The serrations are repeated by the two small chunks of coral and the dried, skeletonized castor-bean leaves. The head of the screw, visible at lower right, can be countersunk and masked with plastic wood.

12

cacti, a surprisingly wide range of woody plants grow under desert conditions. The ghostwood from these scrubby specimens excels in textural beauty. The wind, sand and sun turn out choice pieces for the driftwood-hunter who is game to run the desert's gamut.

From Shops

If you are unable or unwilling to become a prospector, or your diligent efforts consistently bear little fruit, you can still "collect" driftwood. There are countless city and roadside shops, also mail-order firms, with excellent selections of decorative wood awaiting your pleasure (and pocketbook).

For example, along the highway approaches to southern Florida are many "driftwood shops," with pieces piled high on the ground. You can browse to your heart's content. Florida's city shops, too, carry "complete" lines of driftwood masterpieces to enchant the most discriminating. Interesting formations, created by nature and modified and beautified by time and the elements, are carefully displayed. Price tags on some of these items are staggering, although the expense of collecting and conditioning probably justifies them. Boats are employed to bring in the driftwood from small islands several miles from shore where pieces are found in quantity. All sizes, shapes, forms and textures are hauled back and sorted out, to await different processes before being offered for sale.

The answer to a driftwood lover's dream is to suddenly come upon a shop with a huge pile of beautiful gray-white pieces gleaming in the sun. I shall never forget the thrill when I saw such a collection on the ground outside a little shop in Miami Beach. My husband and I had visited all the shops we could find, looking for driftwood that would fit our fireplace wall at home. We wanted just the right piece to swoop over the huge span of crab orchard stone extending from floor to ceiling. Accidentally driving into an unfamiliar street in the city, we found the "perfect" wood, right before our eyes! We could hardly stop the car fast enough.

Hanging just over the doorway of the little shop was the most beautiful piece of driftwood I had ever seen. It was exactly what we wanted—what we had been looking for but had given up hope of ever finding. I fairly flew through the door and stood waiting, almost in a frenzy, until it was my turn to be served. It never occurred to me, as I stood there dreaming of the graceful beauty that would soon adorn my wall, that the marvelous specimen of nature hanging over the shop doorway would never be mine.

Finally my turn came and I announced that the piece of driftwood over the doorway was the one I wanted. The clerk looked at me rather quizzically, perhaps pityingly, and replied: "Lady, I don't think you want that piece. It has just been appraised for five thousand dollars."

As I tried to recover from this blow, my eyes were mercifully attracted to a lovely old mangrove root pushed against a wall. This handsome piece was within our means and today it looks very elegant when the light behind it sheds a soft glow over the fireplace wall.

2. Preparation—Hands On or Off?

To some hobbyists the ideal piece of driftwood is one so beautifully wrought by nature that there is neither need nor possibility of improvement at the hands of man. To others the opposite is true—and the handling or preparation of each branch and root is a big part of their hobby. Still others, of course, move between these two extremes. There are several kinds and methods of alteration, conditioning and refinishing. It's up to you to decide which ones, if any, are necessary or desirable. Just remember this one-two-three routine: one, consider each piece as an individual; two, consider every possibility before starting anything; and three, perform each operation with great care.

Trimming

Sometimes there will be nothing to do but trim the bottom off smoothly in order to mount the piece on a base, or prepare it for placement on a pinholder. (These operations are fully explained in Chapter 3.) Wood found along the seacoast is usually very strong and sturdy with few if any protruding nubs to be taken off. The wood collected around lakes, however, usually has a lot of stubs of branches, or it may carry intact the full growth of small branches (see Plate 9).

For proper balance and proportion, as well as for good grooming, many of these confusing lines will have to be removed. This is a crucial decision. What you do at this point will very likely make or break the piece. Before trimming off branches or nubs, study the piece carefully. Try to visualize how it will look after certain parts have been removed. Then visualize it with other parts pruned off. Do this as often as necessary to explore all possibilities. Once you have decided on the best treatment, work slowly. Recheck the appearance of the piece after each twig or nub is removed. The form of the wood will be affected and the interest of its silhouette will depend on the way it is trimmed. You may even decide that it is necessary to take a section from one place and glue it on in another. Although this is fairly easy to do, care should be exercised to make the final result look entirely natural. If branches are small enough to be broken off rather than sawed or clipped off, the scars will look more natural.

Plates 9 through 15 show a series of procedures in preparing a piece of driftwood for use. Notice how too many lines can confuse and detract from the piece. After the step-by-step procedure, you can see the final results— a design of harmony and unity which could not have been achieved without careful pruning and other preparation.

Cleaning

There is nothing like soap, water, a good stiff brush and plenty of elbow grease to clean a dirty piece of driftwood. A little steel wool will come in handy, too, to help loosen stubborn grime. Once the dirt is cleaned away, the natural color of the wood shows through. A soft brown usually replaces the silvery gray that was evident before scrubbing. Avoid too vigorous scrubbing, for you can destroy this quality. A knife will be required to cut away rotten wood or to dig out particles of decay from angles and crevices.

A gentle brushing or wiping may be the only cleaning necessary for pieces found lodged on top of a heap after being washed ashore, or caught on rocks or brush that

19

prevented them from lying on the ground and becoming grimy. When I find such driftwood, I am reluctant to scrub it for fear of losing the lovely silver patina it has acquired while bleaching in the sun. However, if cleaning is necessary and the silver bloom is rubbed off, the patina might be restored if you leave the wood in the sun for a few weeks, giving it an occasional wetting. If, after this treatment, the gray color isn't sufficiently restored, rub in white chalk. This has proved to be a good artificial restorative.

Sand-blasting is the method used for cleaning driftwood in large quantities for commercial use. In coastal cities where wood is brought in by boatloads from offshore islands, sandblasting is necessary to rid it of any parasites or sea life that may be clinging to it. This treatment does a thorough job of cleaning, since the sand is blown with terrific force against all surfaces. This not only cleans off all residue but also cuts away the coating of silver bestowed by salt water and sun. Sand-blasting also brings back the natural color of various kinds of wood, revealing the beauty of grain that has been hidden by the coat of gray. While visiting several driftwood shops, I discovered this operation to be an expensive one. You will pay a great deal more for wood that has been sand-blasted, but the beauty of color and textural quality

Plate 9. Typical of the decorative wood found along a lake shore, this piece has too many nubby, broken branches.

Plate 10. Another view of the same piece: The addition of accessories and flowers (such as these pear blossoms) merely serves to emphasize the confusing and busy effect caused by the excess of branches poking out at various angles. Some refining art work with a saw is urgently needed.

Plate 11. The refining process begins. A "leg" has already been removed from the base, and one of the unnecessary branches is here being sawed off.

Plates 12 and 13. A pair of progress-report views of the same driftwood. They illustrate a point: A branch that is unattractive in its original position should not be automatically discarded. It

may be just right in some other position. But if it isn't, don't insist on using it somewhere, anywhere, merely to satisfy your frugal instinct.

Plate 14. The sizable two-pronged branch (protruding to the left in Plates 12 and 13) has been relocated; it is now angling outward from the right-hand base of the driftwood. This carefully reasoned bit of pruning and gluing has paid off in much better balance and symmetry. The piece is now ready for a solo display or to provide the backbone for an arrangement.

Plate 15. Here the trimmed and realigned piece of driftwood plays the leading role in a lively arrangement of pear branches, daffodils and tulips.

obtained as a result of this treatment is usually well worth the extra cost.

Once the trimming and cleaning have been accomplished, the next steps of preparation involve the finishing touches. These can be as simple or as elaborate as you choose to make them. A deciding factor will be where and how you plan to use the piece. Equally important are its individual characteristics.

Sanding

For a very fine finish, wood may be sanded, first with coarse sandpaper, graduating to the medium grade, then to fine and on to double-o. An emery cloth may be used to give a still finer finish. A little strong-arm treatment can change the roughest texture to one of soft smoothness. As the grooming continues, the piece will take on a "sculptured look." Its character will change, its individuality will become more distinctive. In a very real sense, you are creating your own sculpture.

Waxing

Some hobbyists prefer to hand-rub and polish their pieces to a fine finish without the aid of wax. This method is satisfactory for those who have the time and patience, and no doubt the satiny finish acquired is worth the effort, but I incline toward all the short cuts I can discover—just so long as they give equivalent results.

The easiest and quickest way I have found to obtain a nice sheen on driftwood is to apply liquid wax with a small paint brush, then buff the surface with a soft cloth. If more sheen is desired, pat on a little paste wax and rub it to a soft mellowness. This will give a very clean, distinctive look. If you wish to retain a lovely gray color, do not do any sanding or waxing.

Staining

To some admirers of nature the thought of artificially coloring a beautifully weathered piece of driftwood is abhorrent. Others stain or dye every piece as a matter of course. Again I say: No blanket rules are possible with driftwood; each piece needs and deserves individual consideration.

There are many avenues open to you. Wood can be stained mahogany, walnut, maple and so on—any color for which there is a wood-stain liquid product available. For professional results, use a high-quality stain. Read and carefully follow the package directions for staining natural wood surfaces. After a thorough drying period, a waxing is advisable to bring back the wood's vitality and

29

to give it a finished look. Polishing to a high sheen will give an extra touch.

Painting

I used to regard as well-nigh sacrilegious any painting of nature's handiwork. But then I gave it a try, and I must admit that some stunning effects can be achieved.

Remember that once a piece of driftwood is painted, its "natural" days are over—so proceed with caution. You can change the first paint color easily enough with another coat, but removal is next to impossible. I suggest that you start with a piece you do not prize too highly. You will be startled to discover the complete change in character that paint will bring about. No matter how insignificant a piece may seem, after it is painted, it takes on new importance and may be used in very dignified compositions. Try tinting your driftwood, for example, to harmonize with a color scheme for a special occasion.

Always use a flat paint—never a high gloss that will give the wood a hard, unnatural finish. Always follow the instructions on the can. Fast-drying water paint is especially easy to work with and gives a soft finish that adds to textural interest rather than detracting from it. The frequent difficulty of obtaining the exact color desired may be overcome by purchasing a small tube of pure chroma to add drop by drop to white paint until the right tint or shade is reached.

Black can be stunning, dramatic and effective, as shown in the arrangement of black and white in Plate 31. This arrangement was created to complement a modern setting where white, accented with black, predominated. A piece of driftwood can also be transformed into a magnificent eye-catcher by applying a coat of gold paint. Gold is used extensively, not only for holiday decorations, but for any occasion demanding elegance. (See the all-gold arrangement in Plate 68.) White is also popular for the Christmas season.

Many colors come in spray-on cans ready for use. These prove to be timesavers—that is, if you can find the desired color in a can. In any case, enjoy your driftwood, with or without paint.

3. Mountings and Supports

A surprising number of flower arrangers—including those of wide experience—have never known the rewards of working with driftwood, even though they greatly admire it. Why?—simply because they do not know how to handle it and have somehow acquired the notion that the whole thing is very complicated. This is certainly not true, as you will soon discover. The mechanics for arranging driftwood—mounting or supporting a piece—are easily accomplished. As far as I am concerned, this "mechanical" work is just about as interesting and enjoyable as the creation of the final composition. Remember that, in general, an arrangement is no better than the mechanics employed in its construction.

The subject of mechanics has been covered again and again in the many books on flower arranging, but in creating driftwood designs a few special techniques are necessary. You should acquire a working knowledge of these, plus deftness in their execution.

32

MOUNTINGS AND SUPPORTS

Mounting

Regardless of the kind of arrangement you are making, or the container you are using, driftwood must be securely mounted. Stability is essential. The larger the piece the more essential is a firm mounting. Take your time and do a good job, or you may come to know the heartbreak of having a beautiful composition topple over the instant you pick it up or turn your back on it.

Usually there is some trimming or sawing to be done at the bottom of the wood before it is mounted, so it will fit smoothly on the base. Study the piece carefully for its interest of line and best possible balance. Hold it at different angles. An easy way to determine where the wood should be sawed is to place it against the edge of a table, as in Plate 16. Hold it at the exact angle at which it is to be mounted and mark this line with a pencil. Then saw through the pencil marking and the bottom will be smooth and level. If this is done correctly, the wood will be ready for mounting without further ado.

There are various methods of mounting driftwood. Each piece has its own requirements. The different ways I will describe are the ones I have found to be effective. Those of you who are experienced with driftwood

Plate 16. It is often necessary to trim a jagged piece of driftwood to give it a wide, flat base on which it will stand at the best angle. The surest way to do this is to hold the piece against the edge of a table at the desired angle, mark it with a pencil (with the table serving as the straight-edge ruler), and then saw along that line.

have probably worked out your own methods. The technique really doesn't matter, so long as it works.

Bases

The best way to mount large, heavy upright pieces is to screw them onto bases that have been cut to the right size and proportion. My bases are made to order by a lumber company, and then I finish them according to the piece of driftwood used. In Plate 116 I have used the wipe-painting technique to finish the base in a lower value of gray so that it will blend with the wood. Allow the paint to remain on for a few minutes, then lightly wipe it off. This gives a soft, natural look to a wood surface and seems to give good textural relationships between an article of driftwood, its base and its surroundings.

Place the wood on the base in the exact spot it is to be mounted. Leave enough space at the back or to one side of the driftwood for a can (I use tuna cans) large enough to hold a needlepoint and water for fresh material. Holding the wood securely in place, mark around it with a pencil, as in Plate 17.

You are now ready to drill holes for the screws. If you can get someone to drill while you hold the wood in position, or vice-versa, you can speed the job by turning the

Plates 17 and 18. If the driftwood has no adequate base (or potential base area) of its own, a base must be provided. Screw mounting is simple and sure. Place the driftwood on the previously prepared base, allowing enough room for a can to hold a needlepoint and water in case the driftwood is to be used with

fresh plant material. Carefully mark the position of the drift-wood. Then, as explained in detail under the subheading Bases in Chapter 3, drill a pilot hole, or holes, through the base and into the driftwood, so a screw may be driven in without splitting the wood.

whole article (with its base) upside down and drilling through the center of the mark from underneath the base and into the driftwood. (See Plate 18.) Otherwise drill through the penciled mark on top of the base. In this case, place the bottom of the driftwood over the drilled holes in the base, and mark the bottom to make sure the holes to be drilled in it will correspond with those in the base. Drill as many holes as necessary for security; one screw will not be sufficient if the piece is large and heavy.

Make sure the screws are long enough to sink deeply into the driftwood so it will be anchored firmly to the base. Countersink the screws into the base to permit it to rest smoothly on any surface and to prevent scratching or marring furniture. Glue a piece of felt to the base if you plan to stand the piece on fine furniture.

Stem Method for Pinholders

For mounting or anchoring smaller, lightweight driftwood on pinholders in arrangements, a different treatment is required. Most driftwood is so hard it is almost impossible to impale it on a pinholder without some mechanical aid. A method I prefer (see Plate 19) is to drill a few holes in the bottom of the wood and drive lengths of woody stems into each hole. (Or strong, straight stems cut from shrubs like privet can be used.) These pegs should be embedded deeply enough in the driftwood to be secure, and should protrude a half-inch to an inch or so. The dowel or shrub wood is soft enough to be easily penetrated by the needlepoints.

These "peg legs" are especially important if the driftwood is to be part of an arrangement that requires water. The pegs will not only keep the bottom of the piece out of the water (preventing rot) but will leave more room on the needles for the anchoring of plant material which may need to be placed on a slant. (See Plate 20.) If you make pegs of fresh wood stems, which may dry out and shrink and thus fall out of the holes, put a few drops of glue into the holes as you insert the pegs. But in the long run you would be wiser to use dried stems, without glue, so that the pegs can be removed to permit the use of the piece on a flat surface.

Styrofoam Bases

Styrofoam or a smiliar product makes an excellent base for a driftwood arrangement. (See Plate 81.) The dowel pegs can be pressed right into the plastic foam without the aid of pinholders. Or you can simply dig a hole in the block of foam to fit your driftwood and press it in, packing floral clay down into the hole around the wood

39

Plates 19 and 20. The Stem Method permits the indirect mounting of driftwood on a needlepoint (driftwood is usually too hard to be pierced by the needles). Drill holes in the base of the piece and firmly insert a dowel-like peg of soft wood into each hole.

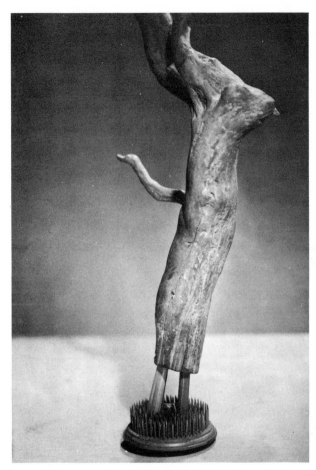

These "stems" elevate the driftwood above the needles. This not only keeps the wood above water but also allows room on the needles to anchor plant material.

to hold it firmly in place. The dug-out pieces of foam can be pressed down over the clay to mask the operation. Styrofoam spray-on paint, which comes in different colors, is also excellent to help conceal the clay. Materials used in the arrangement usually suffice to finish the job of concealment of mechanics.

Temporary Mountings

When you use a stone slab or flat rock as a base for driftwood arrangements, your ingenuity must take over. You cannot drill holes, neither can you dig out little chunks, so you must devise another method. As a rule, stone bases are best used for special occasions, such as a flower show. Their heaviness and roughness make their general use impracticable in the home. In flower shows, where classes are provided for driftwood, bases of rock and stone are most desirable because of their earthiness and natural relationship to driftwood. When you are faced with the problem of setting a good-sized piece of wood on a rock base, then a feasible plan must be worked out.

The problem can be solved with the aid of floral clay or fast-drying glue. Enough clay pressed onto the bottom and around the sides of the wood will hold it to a stone base indefinitely. The clay must be of good quality—not

42

the kind often found at dime stores for the children to play with, but a soft, pliable "professional florist type" such as Posey Klay. This will adhere firmly to both surfaces.

If plant material used in the arrangement does not adequately hide the clay, then use other things which will fit into the design, such as small rocks, pieces of coral or sea shells. These will add interest of form as well as textural value. Quite often I use the beautiful gray lichen found growing on fallen trees or old stumps in the woods, or large curved pieces of bracket fungus. These also have a natural relation to driftwood. (See Plate 109.) Clay was used to support the driftwood in Plate 29, although the base is wood instead of stone or rock. Slabs of bracket fungus not only cover the clay but are used as part of the design, thus serving a dual role.

Fast-drying glue offers a reliable method of mounting driftwood temporarily on a stone or rock base. Apply some glue to the bottom of the wood and to the rock where the wood is to be placed. Wait a few seconds until the glue begins to thicken and gets a little gummy. Then press wood and rock together and hold firmly until the glue sets (only a few moments). Once the glue dries, it holds for a considerable length of time. You can break the bond by giving the base a few hard knocks or jolts. Glue

43

was used to mount the wood on the rock base in Plate 25. Whether or not you use glue for mounting your driftwood, be sure to have it on hand. It comes in handy for repairing broken branches and other emergencies.

Other Props

Free-standing pieces seldom need mechanical aid unless they are slightly off balance. A small piece of wood can be slipped underneath one edge to correct the balance. It can be glued on for permanent support, or screwed to the back as in Plate 8. Sometimes a lump of clay will do the trick and serve to hold the piece firmly for the duration of an arrangement.

On occasion, driftwood sections can be combined to support each other, as in Plate 49. Attractive combinations can be put together temporarily or permanently with the use of clay, glue or screws. Some of my favorite pieces are combinations (Plates 28, 78, 80) and have been joined together by the various methods just described.

Each piece may require a different treatment. If you have a basic knowledge of the essential mechanics necessary for driftwood arranging, new techniques will automatically occur to you.

44

4. Decorative Possibilities

Whether your house is new or old, large or small, contemporary or modern, you can enhance it with the sculptural beauty of driftwood. You can "express yourself" with driftwood. And, as you may have already discovered, driftwood is both durable and adaptable to innumerable decorative uses about the home. In a word, it is practical.

Contemporary and Modern

The ageless beauty of simple, unadorned lines characterizes almost all driftwood and is a major reason for its great popularity. It seems to create an atmosphere of serenity. In decorating our homes this is something we strive for as we select our colors and furnishings. Driftwood "goes with" any concept in decoration that emphasizes the sweep of classic lines.

You and I—modern homemakers—are very much aware of contemporary design. We have developed a feeling for color and texture and are eager to give our homes a special touch. This we can often do, through the simple proportions and clean, uncluttered look of driftwood. The rich mellowness of natural wood tones, or the ascetic silhouette of bleached branches, combines wonderfully well with almost every kind of surroundings.

Driftwood reflects the modern idiom in its sculptural simplicity, its stark, abstract forms, beautiful in the bold structure of angles and the surface variations. Modern design, based on the principle that the suitability of an object creates its own beauty, presents fascinating possibilities for driftwood.

Aid to Busy Homemakers

The use of driftwood in floral arrangements is increasing because there is such affinity between driftwood and flowers. I have devoted a full chapter (Chapter 5) to the subject, for the ease of it makes potential arrangers of almost everyone. Driftwood is ideal for the busy woman who finds her schedule too crowded for much flower arranging in the traditional sense.

Foliage of various kinds—hosta, pothos, aspidistra—can be combined with driftwood for easy and handsome arrangements for the home. And these are long-lasting and so most economical. A few leafy branches from the shrubs in your yard, or cuttings of colorful house plants, will offer fresh ideas. The addition of a few blossoms now and then will give the arrangement a smart pick-up and create an entirely different effect.

Driftwood can be formal or casual, exciting or soothing. Use it as an art piece in the most formal setting; add a figure for a completely satisfying composition. For a pleasing decoration in a modern room where textural interest prevails, what could be better than the texture of weathered wood blending harmoniously with subtle tones of browns and grays that never tire the eyes.

Planters

In contemporary homes with their open spaces, boxes are often built into floors to serve as room-dividers when filled with plant materials. Driftwood is also wonderful for such purposes, giving individuality to the setting and proving to be a very satisfactory decorative element. It is fascinating to watch a lovely philodendron slowly winding its way around a handsome piece of driftwood. You can also bring a fresh attraction to patio or terrace with an individual planter of exotic plants in which driftwood plays the role of ornamental accent.

47

Wall Pieces

A beautifully shaped piece of driftwood mounted on an important wall with a small light behind it also makes an interesting decoration. Or a spotlight can be placed at an angle to create interesting shadows. The effect can be dramatic and much more intriguing than the customary picture hung on the wall.

As accent for a kitchen, study or play room, attach an attractive piece of driftwood firmly to a wall (long screws are best for this), and decorate it with a pot of trailing vines, or one of the small foliage plants. Even artificial vines or flowers look well with driftwood, for today's artificial plant materials have a very alive look. It is their excellent textures which makes it difficult to tell the difference.

Too, when these are used, the chore of watering fresh material is eliminated. You can enjoy the decoration even more because you know that it will be permanently fresh with only an occasional dusting. Decorations of this type are especially attractive on the brick or stone walls of a patio or a closed-in porch.

48

DECORATIVE POSSIBILITIES

Picture Frames for Drama

Although driftwood mounted within a picture frame
might not be called a picture, it can serve the same purpose. One of the most attractive pieces I have seen gave
the feeling of a bird in flight. It was hand-rubbed and
polished to a lovely brownish sheen. A nubby, rough-
textured, beige fabric covering the background, and the
handsome frame surrounding it, complemented the
"bird" in color and texture. The framing of driftwood
arrangements is a challenge. The choice of material will
depend on suitability to the room and, of course, to
your own personal taste.

Dried and Artificial Flower Arrangements

Dried pods and cones, which are available in abundance, are especially compatible with driftwood. Many
good ideas on collecting and on techniques for handling,
wiring and gluing them can be found in Eleanor Van
Rensselaer's book, *Decorating with Pods and Cones.*
The gay colors and forms of artificial flowers, as in Plate
21, appeal to those who like to change designs from time
to time. The photograph shows that instead of gluing
the objects to the background, which is the usual procedure, the flowers have been fastened on with thumb-

49

Plate 21. Here is a long-lasting driftwood picture to decorate a wall. The frame is antiqued gold to blend with the beige of the burlap background. Among the colorful artificial flowers are pink roses and pink camellias with yellow centers.

tacks (obscured by overlapping material), which suggests more depth than fastening them flat against the back. This, of course, also makes it possible for flowers to be easily changed as desired.

Bases for Lamps and Tables

Spectacular pieces of driftwood are magnificently appropriate as bases for lamps and tables. Floor lamps as well as table models prove to be popular "driftwood originals." A glass-top table with an exquisite piece of driftwood for its base is sure to be a matter for conversation. Such pieces add charm and individuality to a room and blend harmoniously with almost any type of furnishings.

You can have bases made to order; or, if you aren't willing to pay the price, you can have fun searching for driftwood and making your own. Often a home workshop will turn into a veritable driftwood shop, and the head of the house will welcome the challenge and the change from his more mundane efforts with chairs, shelves and so forth.

Other Pieces

With a little ingenuity, many other driftwood articles can be made. A popular one is the wall sconce—very lovely, too, as a decorative piece. If you are good at ceramics, you can make attractive ashtrays or flower containers to fit right into the curves and twists of driftwood. Desk-pen sets and book ends are but two of the many ideas that will come to mind once you get started. One idea will serve as a springboard for many others. Since driftwood comes in all shapes and sizes, it will not be too difficult to find a piece to fit the place in your home which will be benefited by the charm that driftwood gives.

Driftwood for Children

Pieces resembling birds and animals make welcome decorations for a child's room. Put your imagination to work. Better still, let the children create for themselves. With a little supervision and guidance from you, they can have the thrill of creating something beautiful. With some carving here and there—perhaps a few lines penciled in to make a face more obvious—and the addition of "button eyes," you will see a driftwood animal come to life. Such pieces can be a source of great pleasure to youngsters, especially if they happen to be shut in for a while.

Part II
THE ART

5. Driftwood in Flower Arrangements

Distinction and originality are built into every piece of driftwood. In each there are forms and textures that present unlimited artistic possibilities.

In our efforts to achieve distinction, we flower arrangers seek the new and unusual. The designs of others may inspire us, but unless we project our own thoughts and feelings into our work, we fall short of achieving our goal—true originality. Isn't the winning of prizes or praise secondary to that?

When we create a floral design we create art, and in all good art there is a dimension or element which gives life to a design, portrays a mood or tells a story. With driftwood these possibilities are easily achieved and, since no two pieces are alike, originality is made easy for you. Once you become aware of driftwood's many potentials, imagination will urge you into action.

Plate 22. Setting a rhythmic pattern, this driftwood supplies the basic structure for the design. Spires of bromeliad foliage direct attention to the low center of interest, made up of echeveria and staghorn fern. The bird figurine in the background adds depth and emphasizes the rhythm. The subdued green of the plant material is in harmony with the soft brown of the branches.

Plate 23. Without a figure, although one would not be amiss, the same piece of driftwood (in Plate 22) can be dramatic with a simple spring arrangement of white tulips with gray pussy willows to stress the rhythm.

Plate 24. The gray-green of dried eucalyptus and sea-grape leaves give a different effect with the same versatile piece of driftwood. The brown-beige toned Chinese warriors intensify the rhythm (see Chapter 7). One figure is elevated (secured with clay on a nub of wood) to give the design better balance.

Plate 25. A contorted piece of decorative wood shares the spotlight in this study of lotus seed pods and sprigs of laurel foliage. The driftwood is set firmly on the stone base with glue. A small bit of moss, placed at the base of the wood to cover any sign of mechanics, also adds texture to the design. The featured figure of a Chinese gentleman contributes interest and balance. The lotus pods are gray on top and brown underneath, picking up the same colors in the figure, the wood and the stone base.

Plate 26. The same brown-colored driftwood, set into a plow disc (for the procedure, see Chapter 3), plays the leading role in a fruit and vegetable arrangement. Creamy white garlic blossoms form the top lines. Young, chartreuse-hued hydrangeas are transitional elements to the grapes, apple and two cucumbers.

Plate 27. Believe it or not, this is the same piece of driftwood as in Plate 26—with a new base. Temporarily attached with clay to a heavy section of wood, it provides a strong structure for this jungle rhythm design, which I call "Bongo Flora." Pale pink rhododendrons pick up the darker value of color in the drums. (Figures by Fred Press.)

Different Every Time

Even though your driftwood collection is small, you achieve distinction each time you use the same piece in a different manner. Examine Plates 22 through 27; although the same two pieces of wood have been used more than once, the designs are entirely different.

Driftwood, with its many varied forms, is a challenging medium to the floral artist—challenging because it is a relatively unexplored field, a new door behind which lies an extravagant range of potential beauty. You will find that wave-washed, weather-worn pieces have special charm and appeal (Plates 108 and 123), while the graceful flowing lines of others will inspire you to new creativity (Plates 53, 90 and 95).

Guiding Principles

When we use driftwood artistically with flowers, we are, or should be, guided by the same basic principles that govern all forms of art. These have been expounded in many books on flower arranging, and I am sure you are already aware of their importance. Actually, the construction of a driftwood design is basically the same as that of any flower arrangement, since we employ the same fundamentals. The main difference is that drift-

62

wood, being so dominant, usually controls the design. Once you understand that, your driftwood efforts are more assured.

Framework Is Important

As in any good arrangement, one of the first considerations of driftwood-floral designing is the framework or skeleton. It differs from the usual procedure in flower arranging in which the framework is established by plant material within the concept of a certain style or pattern. Because of its strong linear form, driftwood establishes not only the frame, which dictates the style or plan, but usually plays the stellar role and controls the internal structure as well. Versatility of design lies within the imagination and ingenuity of the arranger.

Although the three-dimensional contours of driftwood are adequate to establish the skeleton, set the pattern and suggest the compositional scheme, this alone will not assure a successful design. As you build an arrangement, keep in mind that every detail of material, each blossom, leaf or stem should be placed to emphasize the driftwood's distinctive form, to add variety and depth to the design but never to clutter or obscure the wood. (See Plates 77, 90 and 92.)

63

Scale, Proportion, Balance

Since driftwood is usually the predominating element of the design, you must make certain that it is in good scale, proportion and balance. Of course, this is true of any good design, but I can assure you it is not always easy to cope with the domineering influence of driftwood unless you keep before you a constant sense of these values.

In selecting driftwood for an allotted space or container, scale or size should be well considered. Because of its solidity, a piece of decorative wood gives a strong sense of visual weight. In order for other elements of the design not to be overpowered, the size of the piece should be in harmony with other parts of the design as well as with the intended surroundings. No matter how beautiful a piece of oversized driftwood may be, you must either find a properly spacious spot for it or be willing to cut it down to more suitable dimensions.

Whenever I find a lovely but too-large piece that I can't bear to cut, I lay it aside until I find just the right use for it. Maybe it will go to a friend to be used in a planter, to be mounted on a wall, or simply kept for the sheer joy of looking at it—any excuse to save its beauty

64

Plate 28. The natural gap in the center of this coastal wood prevents visual heaviness. The vertical piece is attached to the lower horizontal section with screws. Effective lighting increases the airy feeling of the eucalyptus, euonymus and Fugi chrysanthemums. The yellow flowers and green foliages complement the brown of the sand-blasted wood.

Plate 29. Well-spaced branches furnish interest for the linear form of this brown-toned driftwood in its use with flowers. The piece is temporarily established with floral clay on the smooth flat base. Handsome sections of gray, brown-marked bracket fungus conceal the clay and provide necessary weight at the base. The three stems of beige-centered, red-tipped spoon chrysanthemums could be replaced by other plant materials for a quick change of effect.

Plate 30. The sinuous "outrigger" not only helps to make this piece self-supporting but also gives a Hawaiian feeling to the asymmetrical arrangement of dahlias with clipped and natural castor-bean foliage. A pincup holder placed in the back holds water for the fresh flowers. The dahlias are a light rose hue in the center, graduating to darker values at the outer petals. This picks up the tones of bronzy foliage and brown wood.

Plate 31. A coat or two of paint can transform a commonplace piece of driftwood into a notable ornament. Here flat black paint dramatizes the wood and makes it a perfect background for the large white chrysanthemums and castor-bean leaves. A chunk of black-painted wood underneath provides support at the best angle.

Plate 32. Unusual twirls and curves of driftwood form the basic structure and heighten the interest in this arrangement of artificial dahlias in a modern black container. The dahlias are orange-red; the wood, gray.

Plate 33. A soaring branch, securely glued to a great section of
weathered wood, supplies a good vertical line for this spring
arrangement of wild azaleas. The rich salmon pink of the flowers
is lovely against the gray wood.

Plate 34. In this essentially oriental composition, the ornamental black holder and the Japanese wicker basket appear as one unit with the elongated, tapering sweep of the driftwood, the earth-seeking leafy branch, and the clean white chrysanthemums.

Plate 35. In an Early American jar, two pieces of driftwood make
a strong framework for a design with red geraniums and their
own foliage, and three daffodil leaves. The flower and foliage
colors are pleasing with the browns of wood and pottery.

Plate 36. Grotesquely angled and curved wood creates an unusual silhouette for this arrangement of three chrysanthemums and one large castor-bean leaf. The driftwood is supported in the container by a molded base of floral clay. The dark brown band around the rim of the gray-green bowl repeats the driftwood's hue. Pleasing color is supplied by the pale yellow of the chrysanthemums and the bronze of the leaf.

Plate 37. Through judicious pruning, this piece of driftwood suggests the Japanese triangle of heaven-earth-man. Green eucalyptus and white chrysanthemums complete the asymmetrical design. Distinction is contributed by the figure container and the magnificent slab of polished burl.

Plate 38. Towering and top-heavy, this branch could not stand unaided. Screws securely fasten it to the base, allowing the graceful linear curves to accent an arrangement of yellow-green bells-of-Ireland, lavender-rose asters and dark green loquat foliage.

Plate 39. A substantial, free-standing and yet wonderfully delicate unit is achieved by this unusual treatment of two sections
of driftwood. One is perfectly balanced on the other to form a
basket for pink, yellow-centered camellias and rich green podo-
carpus. The biege-brown of the wood sets off the colors of flowers
and foliage.

from the saw. The appeal of such pieces is quite over-whelming at times.

Proportion, too, must be considered if there is to be unity and an over-all pleasing effect. By that I mean proportion to the space the driftwood is to occupy, to the base it may be mounted on, and to any other elements used in the design. Good design is always unified, and proportion is essential to unity.

In driftwood designing balance is of paramount importance. The design's structural solidity, on which its balance will depend, must be assured. If it has been established on a sturdy foundation, you are off to the right start. Because of its contour, a driftwood design will often be asymmetrically balanced. The correct placement of plant material, and accessories, if used, will provide interest and variety as well as the necessary visual weight.

With the proper scale, proportion and balance, plus security of mechanics, flower arranging with driftwood should be pure pleasure. If you have difficulty in working out your design, stop and check those three values. Chances are you have lost sight of one of them.

Rhythm

Rhythm is the heartbeat of your arrangement, bringing to it vitality and grace. The well-planned design will

77

have a sense of motion that leads the eye with such freedom of movement that the observer will be able to take in all the details comfortably at first glance. The sweeping curves of driftwood, which are one of its chief assets, form a natural rhythm for your designs. (See Plates 53, 95 and 116.)

Dominance and Contrast

Although a strong piece of driftwood is naturally the dominant element in the arrangement, it is possible to destroy this powerful effect, to reduce it with plant material. I have seen this done many times, and inevitably with a loss of beauty in all elements. Plant material should feature and dramatize the wood, not hide it.

To be sure, the arrangement must have contrast—contrast of form, color and texture to bring harmony and unity to the design. There is no dearth of adaptable foliage and floral material. The neutral gray or brown tones of driftwood, so pleasantly easy on the eye, are delightfully compatible with almost any flower color you might choose. Soft, subdued colors of plant material blend yet contrast with the mellowness of wood tones. Contrasts of strong, bold colors are stimulating, yet they, too, are pleasing with driftwood. Smooth textures of petal and

78

leaf played against rough textures of driftwood bring life and interest to the design.

Figurines—animals, birds, human figures—offer additional contrast. In fact, driftwood with figurines can be completely satisfying without the use of any plant material.

Plate 40. A single, *natural* piece of wood of unbelievably intricate formation gives a strange sense of motion to this composition of white chrysanthemums in a tall white container. An unnoticeable prop holds the piece firmly in the vase. Dark loquat leaves complete the design.

Plate 41. Slim and angular, this piece of driftwood gives verve
to a basically simple arrangement of two pink roses—one bud
and one bloom. The teakwood intensifies the oriental feeling.

Plate 42. Like a bolt of lightning, this branch zigzags down and seems to explode in a white flash of spring flowers—tulips and narcissus. The lines of the pussy-willow branches and tulip foliage contribute to the startling effect.

Plate 43. Clever lighting works magic on this composition, giving visual impact to the powerful lines of the wood. A flowering branch of wild plum in a sparkling glass bowl completes the composition.

Plate 44. Vibrant with life and anticipated action, this naturalistic creation would fascinate a very young as well as an adult
audience. The mother bird, apparently about to return to her
nest, adds glistening blue tones to the duller blue of the eggs, the
pink of the apple blossoms and the harmonious browns of the
driftwood and base.

Plate 45. Considerably more stylized than the woodsy scene in Plate 44, this vertical design has a different effect, with the rosy-breasted robin figurine playing a major role. In harmony are the grays of container and driftwood, the aquamarine of the eggs and the green of boxwood twigs.

Plate 46. This illustrates how driftwood can enhance and yet not dominate a design. The curves of the wood are in contrast here to the sharp vertical lines of a century plant. Ti leaves, chartreuse chrysanthemums, gray-green periploca or silk-vine seed pods and yellow-green agave spikes complete the picture.

Plate 47. A twisting yet essentially horizontal line of driftwood is set off by a contrasting vertical arrangement of pussy willow and pittosporum. If your dinner table is large, this would look well on it, the smooth waxed surface compatible with the finer polish of the table. A fruit arrangement is also effective with this ranging branch.

Plate 48. This is a story-telling piece for all ages. The brown driftwood, fastened to brown tree burls with floral clay is in tune with the brown-colored, early spring buds of buckeye. But the small squirrel figures are the heart of the setting. Gray lichen conceals the pincup holder for water that keeps the buckeye fresh.

Plate 49. Perfectly balanced, one on the other, these two pieces illustrate the limitless possibilities of driftwood construction. Diagonal placement of the airy sprays of wild pink azalea breaks the weighty horizontal crossing of the gray wood.

Plate 50. A swooping branch is set off by an interesting container —a green-painted plow disc. Floral clay is the anchor. Yellow daffodils and green pittosporum leaves are decorative but not essential elements in the composition.

6. Four Seasons with Driftwood

In striving for originality and novelty in our flower arranging, we often fall into the trap of overlooking the obvious. What could be more under our noses than the four seasons? And although they move along in the same order every year, they are always fresh and different. Have you ever known a spring that was exactly like the spring of the preceding year? Or a summer, a fall or a winter? There is an automatic factor of differentness waiting to aid the arranger who merely uses the flowers, foliages and fruits of the current season in driftwood compositions. We enjoy nature's variety of seasons and the flowers that come with each. It's a simple matter to carry that over into our arranging. And it is a challenge to symbolize the variations in the changing seasons—a challenge that should have strong appeal for a creative person.

With Spring Flowers

After the long months of winter, the budding evidence of spring is joyously welcome. From the first crocus to the early daffodils, from the unfurling leaves to the swelling buds of flowers and branches, we watch Mother Nature as she breathes warmth and new life into the dormant plants about us. At times we force plants into bloom in the house ahead of schedule, so eager are we for a change.

With the renewed interest and vitality that each spring brings, we plunge excitedly into the glories of planning new driftwood-floral arrangements. As spring bursts forth and we are engulfed by the beauty about us, thoughts for many new arrangements surge through our minds. Not only for the spring do we plan, but for other seasons of the year. As blossoms reach their peak, it is time to dry them for use in winter designs. Spring stirs budded branches into life. Their flowing curves inspire flights of imagination as they slowly take on color. Their graceful curves can add rhythmic harmony to our driftwood patterns.

Abundance and Restraint

During the wonderful spring months we bask in fresh beauty. We fill our homes with the riotous color found in abundance in the garden. With well-intentioned enthusiasm, we yield to the temptation to try each lovely plant we have grown, reveling in exciting color combinations. It is difficult to keep from adding more than is necessary—but always remember that restraint is one of the essentials of good design.

Simplicity is a reliable touchstone. No matter how great the desire to put in one more lovely flower or leaf, we must practice control. This does not mean that all driftwood designs must be alike in sparseness of floral material. Simplicity can also be achieved with the lavish use of flowers and leaves if a design is properly executed. Some interpretations will require much more material than others, as you will note in the designs in this book. These are thoughts for spring and for all the seasons. Your own knowledge of design and good taste in the selection of both driftwood and plant material will rule your creations.

With Summer Flowers

In no time at all the briskness of spring gives way to the long days of summer. School is out, bringing the hurly-burly of children underfoot again. These are the days when a busy mother finds driftwood compositions a joy. With a minimum of time and effort, she can place a few flowers with a piece of driftwood for a delightful accent in the home. The framework is permanently established, and fresh material can be quickly changed from

93

time to time. Pleasing results are always assured, for there are so many different kinds of garden material available (or inexpensive florist material, if you're not a home owner).

The informality of contemporary living influences our interpretation of the free and easy moods of summer. You can subtly capture these moods with curving, leafy branches that replace the flowering ones of spring (Plate 51). With the passing of daffodils, tulips, hyacinths, forsythia and quince, you can find other flowers in the summer garden. The characteristics of summer growth are quite different from those of spring, but just as appealing. The rounded forms, sprays and young growth of fruit will inspire you to create many appropriate designs for summer.

With Daylilies and Annuals

Daylilies, the "queens for a day," are naturals with driftwood, and very versatile, too. Flowers range from those with the rough texture and harsh colors of the roadside varieties to the magnificent hybrid daylilies so beautifully shaped in porcelain-like textures. (See Plate 76.) For full enjoyment, bring in one or two different varieties each day and arrange with driftwood. For

94

Plate 51. Leafy branches and two gnarled sections of wood, joined with screws, form a free-standing structure and a naturalistic setting for the Chinese figure. The open-centered vertical piece repeats the pose of the figure. (This decorative wood was also used as the backbone of a flower design in Plate 28.)

Plate 52. Unusual containers are often created by arrangers. Here the inverted shade of an old brass lamp serves as the bowl, and the base of the lamp provides an ornamental footing. Supported on a needlepoint holder by the Stem Method (Chapter 3), the brown-toned driftwood sets off the salmon zinnias and green honeysuckle foliage.

Plate 53. The success of this design depends on a partnership of the major elements of driftwood and plant material. Yellow-gold marigolds blend with variegated calla-lily foliage, and these two, in turn, bring out the tones of driftwood and base.

Plate 54. The cresting of an ocean wave is suggested by this dynamic swirl of free-standing driftwood. Late summer colors —orange, orange-red, and bronze—are featured in the spotted lilies, castor-bean seed pods and an acorn squash.

Plate 55. Ugliness and beauty are companions in this gouged
and twisted piece of natural sculpture. Actually it is not entirely
the work of nature. To increase terminal interest, a twirled
length of branch was glued to the top of the large section. Bits
of gray lichen cover the joining seam and look like natural
growth on the wood. Pale yellow, smooth-petaled daylilies re-
lieve the rather forbidding aspect of the piece.

Plate 56. The units of this composition seemed made for each other, especially the driftwood and container. The wood cradles the composition of fruits, flowers, vegetables and foliage. The arm of wood sweeping to the right continues and balances the line of soaring, multicolored bird-of-paradise flowers (strelitzia). The loop of wood unifies the design of orange-red persimmons, berried pyracantha, variegated croton and green to orange-red peppers.

Plate 57. Two bulky parts can make a graceful whole, as in this combination of heavy driftwood on one side and a bountiful composition of fruit, flowers and leaves on the other. The rosy hue of the zinnias is echoed in apple and pears. A strong note of yellow is supplied by the lemon and bananas, but it is softened by the green and grayish hues of the grapes and rosettes of echeveria. Honeysuckle branches are added for grace.

Plate 58. Two pieces of driftwood, temporarily joined with floral clay, form the structure for this arrangement of banana blossoms and water grass with artificial fruit. The figure, although detached in space from the design, is a vital part of it.

contrast, try smooth-textured hemerocallis with rough-textured wood, and vice versa.

As summer glides along, annual flowers come more and more to the fore, led by the reliable zinnias and marigolds (Plates 52, 53). These two can be real summer stars if you have remembered to plant them instead of rejecting them as too old-fashioned and common to bother with. Many of the new hybrids produce exotic forms and colors, interesting to work with. Because of their long-blooming season and lasting quality, as well as the varied color combinations obtainable, you will not tire of using them even after the early fall flowers arrive.

Toward the end of summer, as the garden shows signs of barenness, we become increasingly eager for another season. With aid from the florist, we enjoy exotic imports and greenhouse-grown flowers for in-between fill-ins until fall flowers begin to bloom. Asters and early chrysanthemums are readily obtainable and work in well with summer foliages, such as castor bean and cannas, which last until frost.

Fruits and Vegetables for Autumn

Autumn days, the days of the harvest, bring new sources of inspiration for driftwood arrangements. Fruits

103

and vegetables offer many possibilities with their wide range of forms, textures and brilliant colors. Beauty is where we find it, and certainly it is found in the marvelous variety of autumn's bounty.

Driftwood, because of its versatility, can be used in pleasant combination with any plant material. Special satisfaction, however, awaits the arranger who can capture the zesty moods of fall in distinctive designs of fruits and vegetables. (See Plate 56.) Such an arrangement can be as stimulating as next year's fashion and as refreshing as an April shower. Geometric and abstract forms are found in the structural solidity of vegetables and fruits. And, of course, these combine beautifully with flowers.

The use of fruits and vegetables with driftwood is no different from the creation of other designs. You are still working with forms, textures and color, and must follow the same principles if you are to obtain harmonious effects. Group similar forms or kinds together instead of mixing them. Contrasting forms, colors and textures used in different amounts will provide ample variation. Vary the sizes of forms—some small, some medium, some large—just as you do in standard flower arranging. When using two or more pieces of the same or of different kinds of fruit, let the rounded end, the blossom end, of one piece show in contrast to the pointed end of an-other, thus adding more interest than if all were placed uniformly. Any degree of variety will add interest.

Also, since texture and color, as well as form, are equally important to the design, you should give con-siderable thought to your color patterns and surface tex-tures. An orderly placement will provide necessary tran-sition and create an easy flow of rhythmic movement through the design.

With Dried Materials

As the brilliant autumn fades into the somberness of winter, dried flowers take the spotlight. Often a com-bination of dried and fresh plant material will have a special charm.

Since colonial days, dried flowers and foliage have been important in home decoration. Old-fashioned dried arrangements, which consisted mostly of buxom bunches of pampas grass and seed pods, kept the busy homemaker even busier with constant cleaning up of fuzz and seeds. Today's dried arrangements, being better designed and constructed, are not only functionally dec-orative but much easier to care for. Also, modern drying methods assure an almost indefinite—and very lifelike—future for dried blooms in driftwood compositions.

Plate 59. Chunky yet graceful, this piece of driftwood serves both as container and setting for the fruits and flowers. The important vertical line is actually a branch attached to the heavy base piece. The colorful red zinnias harmonize with the tints of the artificial bananas, apples and apricots.

Plate 60. A boat-shaped slab of bark holds an appropriately angled cargo, a summer arrangement of callicarpa berries, dahlias and unripened scuppernongs (grapes). On a waxed or glass-topped table, without the metal stand, the boat effect would be even more pronounced. The young grapes are yellow-green, as are the tips of the callicarpa twigs, but the berries graduate down toward lavender-purple to match the dahlias.

Plate 61. Securely braced by small wood pieces in a huge plow disc (anchored by lichen-camouflaged floral clay), this three-and-one-half-foot section of gray driftwood adequately supports the load of dark, red-purple blossoms and small green bananas. Tall yellow-green pandanus leaves reinforce the design.

Plate 62. A gyrating, protruding arm of driftwood gives balance to this arrangement of artificial fruit and colored wheat in a modern black jug. The three-legged stand plays an important role in elevating the container, so that the branch has plenty of air space.

Plate 63. An obvious but not unnatural-looking joining of two driftwood branches (with glue) produces a piece that provides vertical accent for a winter composition of dried materials. The ribs of the burned palmetto leaves accentuate the design. The round forms of bracket fungus (brown in front, beige in back) create the center of interest and repeat the curve in the wood at this point. Brown thistles and canna foliage stress the sere and withered look of winter.

Plate 64. A three-part lesson—in scale and line and texture—is offered here, and the figures of the bears are vital to all three. Their furry texture is in contrast to the roughness of the driftwood. Their size—the appearance of being dwarfed by their surroundings—emphasizes the imposing height and breadth of line. Dried castor-bean foliage has been trimmed into round forms, repeating the circular movements in the wood. The figures also serve as anchor where vertical and horizontal lines meet.

Plate 65. A heavy, oddly gnarled and knotted lump of driftwood is foundation for an arrangement of dried canna leaves and spikes of mullein. Without plant material, this free-standing unit makes an attractive ornament.

Plate 66. The texture of this partly burned piece of wood, running horizontally, is reflected in each yucca pod in the cluster. Curled palm spathes, forming a vertical structure, are also in good textural relationship. Brown is the color theme.

New styles in dried designs have broken further with tradition, as in Plate 63. The relationship of driftwood and dried flowers is a natural one. Both, in fact, are dried plants. Perhaps you have never thought of driftwood as being plant material at all, but rather a wood form. Actually, of course, at one time it was fresh plant material. Consequently, in its natural state, regardless of its size, shape or form, it is dried plant material. Its sculptural beauty is vividly shown in Plate 63; the design consists of driftwood, burned palm (not only dried but burned, too), thistles, canna foliage and bracket fungus. What fresh materials could possibly produce such textural variation? What could be more distinctive than those misshapen burned palms? In Plate 64 the piece of decaying wood and the trimmed castor-bean foliage (one stem dried on an angle and placed backward for added dimension) present a fascinating study in texture. The dried, brittle leaves relate perfectly to the wood.

Improved methods of preserving plant material, by which color and surface quality can be retained, make it easy for you to have the color scheme of your choice in dried arrangements.

Combining Fresh and Dried

The special appeal of combining fresh and dried floral material in a driftwood design lies in the fact that varia-

114

tions of interest can be obtained in color, form and texture merely by changing the fresh material. This alters the whole appearance. In Plates 71 and 74, note the fresh and dried arranged together, and how the center of interest could be changed with ease without disturbing the fairly permanent framework.

Harmonious relationship of materials must be considered with special care in this type of arrangement. If you have thoughtfully weighed the principles of dominance and contrast in working out your design, there will be unity and not discord. The rough and krinkly textures of driftwood and dried materials, of course, will form the dominant textural interest. The fresh material will play its role in offering contrast of texture as well as form and color. Working out compositions of driftwood with dried and fresh materials for the winter months is a challenge both stimulating and relaxing.

Plate 67. Light and shadow gives additional dimension to this formation of wood. Balanced in a ceramic container, its texture and tan-brown tones blend with the dried globe thistle, canna leaves and the two small sprays of loquat buds at the base.

Plate 68. An angular branch glued to a three-pronged fragment of root gives the effect here of a driftwood ballet with a coat of gold to give a gay, glittery air. Gold-hued artificial material is placed around the wood to develop the design from every direction. This is a requisite in a table centerpiece.

Plate 69. Two balanced sections of wood, one bracing the other, form the base and half of the vertical interest here. Completing the picture, in a blend of browns, grays and greens, are clipped palmettos and swirls of dried roadside plant material.

Plate 70. A twisted root, set upright in a metal stand on a polished wood burl, makes an imposing foundation for a composition of dried and fresh material. A pincup to hold water is anchored in the top of the wood. Fresh, rose-lavender asters backed by bronzy galax leaves are a bright spot between dried, purple liatris and dark purple artificial grapes.

Plate 71. Red-orange tithonia blossoms give a "below the equator" tone to this permanently anchored driftwood structure. Clipped, dried palmettos rise from the dark green loquat foliage to balance the figure with the chartreuse banana.

Plate 72. Central bulk and diagonal thrust of the driftwood focus attention on a study of dried, gray-green eucalyptus and fresh, pale pink gladiolus accented by shiny green loquat leaves.

Plate 73. A twisted branch glued to a free-standing knot (procedure shown in Plates 5 and 6) forms the essential upright line
here. Pod-topped poppy stems match the curves of the branch,
and yellow, green-centered spider chrysanthemums add airy
grace. Gray pods pick up the gray of wood and stone base.

Plate 74. Curved branches spiraling out in all directions set off the dried bells-of-Ireland (in pale green) and poplar blossoms (in green and beige). Loquat leaves add substance at the base. Concealed behind the free-standing driftwood is a pincup for water.

7. Figures with Driftwood

If you would give a touch of life, a sense of motion to your designs, do not overlook the value of figures, either featured or used as accessories. Figurines, or figures, offer great opportunity to express a personal taste. The right selection can transform a mediocre design into one of distinction. There is no limit to the variety of figures available. They are made of wood, metal, glass, plaster and other materials, in many forms, styles and colors. Their versatility provides never-ending pleasure. They can unify and soften, suggest an atmosphere and bring new dimension to a design. They can be the main element or the one perfect accent, or give depth and charm to a quiet background.

As Accessories

An accessory may be defined as an article or device which contributes subordinately to an effect; an accompaniment that adds effectiveness. A good arranger is discriminating in selecting figurine accessories so they will add to, and not interfere with, the effect of the design.

Selection

As arrangers—whether experienced or not—we know that a knowledge and observation of design principles is a prerequisite to success. And there is equal reason to follow through with the same principles in selecting and using figures or other accessories with our driftwood designs.

It should go without saying that an accessory ought never be used just for its own sake, because it is interesting or beautiful. If it is not going to add to the effectiveness of the design, leave it out. If you are reasonably sure it will be an asset, then plan its use while working out your idea. If, after the composition is completed, you discover that your original idea was not a good one, be wise enough to admit it and start over, either with a different figure or a different idea, or both.

The figure must have meaning and relationship to the other materials in an arrangement. In Plate 75, there is no question of the effectiveness of the accessory. The scene suggests a "challenge to the finish." What would it be without the figure of the bull? He brings the whole thing to life, with much anticipated action. An entirely

125

different atmosphere is evoked in Plate 118. Without the rocks and cross the composition would have little impact. With them, the story of Easter morning and the empty tomb is vividly portrayed. In each case, it is easy to realize that omission of the accessories would have left the composition less interesting as well as less well-balanced.

When planning a design, try to envision the contribution of the accessory. If the use of the figure is a last-minute afterthought, chances are the design will be better off without it.

Though we know now that an accessory can aid the design and offer opportunity for originality—this still is not enough. If there is to be unity, the accessory must also harmonize in scale, color and texture.

Scale

The actual size of the object used as an accessory should not be obviously too large, or too small. If it is too large, the arrangement itself may be overpowered; if too small, it will detract from the design.

It is comparatively easy to discern the right scale and proportion of a figure for driftwood arrangements. Of course, scale can be worked out mathematically, but visual dexterity usually can be developed to a high degree. The Chinese water boy in Plate 76 is in good scale, the right size for a boy in relation to the "driftwood tree" near which he is standing. In Plate 77 the actual size as well as the brawniness of the horse is well related to the heavy twisted "laurel tree" above him. The bird in Plate 78 is of pleasing scale with the other elements of the design.

You can use figures that are obviously small in scale to emphasize a point, as I have done in Plates 103 and 111. Here the insignificance of man and beast in the vast expanse of Nature's outdoors is evident. On the other hand, if a particular figure is desirable for a certain design and is too small for good scale, it can be elevated or otherwise given prominence. Alternatively, a second figure may be added to give pleasing proportion and results, as in Plates 24 and 82.

Color and Texture

The close relationship of any object's color and texture makes it almost impossible to separate these elements, or to select an object for one without considering the other. For practical purposes, the two must be considered simultaneously. It may be an easy matter to find the right color or the right texture, but not so easy to find an appropriate accessory that offers both the color

127

Plate 75. Powerful movement marks every rugged line of this realistic design. The great mass of jagged wood towers over, but does not dwarf, the magnificent charging bull. Curled and twisted poinciana seed pods reiterate the curves and color of the brown figure. Saw-toothed spears of a century plant build up the mood and help to relate the driftwood to the earth-like covering of ground moss.

Plate 76. The brown and beige figurine of a Chinese fisherman, shown in another setting in Plate 51, here enhances a design of graceful driftwood, yellow daylilies (both buds and blooms) and loquat foliage. The wood is screwed to the base.

Plate 77. A curiously contorted piece of sand-blasted, tan-colored driftwood makes a dramatic setting for the excited figure of the stallion. The swirls of the wood first draw the eye upward to the mountain-laurel blossoms, then swing it down to the figure. The almost-white flowers match the mane and tail of the otherwise brown horse.

Plate 78. The joining (with glue) of a rhythmic branch and a small chunky piece of wood creates a driftwood formation that serves as container as well as linear structure for an arrangement of white, yellow-centered camellias. The bird, with white-tipped wings, is a suitable accessory. The sand-blasted driftwood has a smooth brown texture which blends with the smoothness of the other elements.

Plate 79. Here is an example of the use of an essential accessory. Without the angular bird, this driftwood design of castor-bean pods and foliage and daffodil leaves would lack lateral balance. Lively color appeal is provided by the rose-red pods, yellow-green daffodil spears, bronze castor-bean leaf, black figure and gray wood.

Plate 80. Two oddly formed pieces of wood make a good unit when firmly joined with screws, and the carved tropical bird suits the setting. Calla-lily foliage, rose-colored celosia and gray wood are in harmony with the bird's black head and mahogany body.

Plate 81. Gold-painted driftwood, rubbed with colored chalk, associates well with a gaudy, coral-tinted bird, artificial line material and chartreuse Christmas-tree balls. The block of Styrofoam, sprayed a bronzy gold, completes the stylized holiday design.

Plate 82. Two pieces of gray driftwood, joined where they stand on the base, frame a design of lavender-purple asters and chrysanthemums. Bromeliad spears accentuate the curve of the wood. Small purple thistle pods add to the color harmony. Smooth ti leaves supply contrast of texture. The statuette—a figure of spring—is elevated in the design for better balance. The dress picks up the floral hues.

and texture desired. The rewards, however, are worth the search.

Coarse textures of driftwood quite often demand much coarser textures in accessories than might otherwise have been used. However, it all depends on the finish of the wood and the textural interest you are seeking.

Contrasting textures, when well planned, add interest and variety, contributing to the character of the design (see Plate 79 for an example). The smooth textures of the bird and the Peruvian daffodil foliage are in arresting contrast to the roughness of the driftwood and coarseness of the castor beans.

Light reflected by the smooth surfaces emphasizes the textural quality of the coarser surfaces which absorb the light. The coloring of the bird, carved from a cow's horn, is predominantly black, with tracings of grayish white which pick up the dull gray tones of the driftwood. The green of the Peruvian daffodil foliage is picked up in the top castor-bean pod where a gradual change of color begins, flowing gently, as it darkens, into the lower pod and dark bronze leaf below.

The nubby material underneath repeats the brown tones of the plant material and the soft brown discernible in the grayish brown driftwood. The compatibility of contrasting textures, the harmonious relationship of colors and the placement of the figure for lateral balance result in a unity of design.

In Plate 25, colors and texture are more closely related. Although the surface quality of the figure, a Chinese gentleman, is smooth (but much less refined than that of the bird), the heavy folds of his robe, his hefty form and brown color are qualities that make this figure much more suitable for the ruggedness of this design than the more delicate bird would be. The strong piece of wood and the heavy rock base demand a sturdy figure. The rock and dried lotus pods both have brown and gray coloring, blending perfectly with the brown of the wood and figure. The laurel foliage and moss at the base of the driftwood give a subtle touch of naturalness which helps to soften and unify, but they are so subordinated to the stronger elements that they are hardly noticeable.

Selecting colors and textures of figures and other accessories for driftwood designs involves the same thoughtful consideration you give to any flower arrangement. The greatest difference is that the strong character of driftwood more often demands greater strength in accessories.

Figures Featured

Among the definitions of "feature" are: star billing; a special attraction; prominent; distinctive.

In order to rate star billing, a figurine must be truly distinctive. It may not always be beautiful but it certainly should be sufficiently outstanding to demand and deserve maximum attention.

When a figure is to be featured, then the composition must be planned especially for it. It definitely must be used in such a manner that the design would not be complete without it. It should be so prominent, attractive or fascinating that it will be the motivating force around which the other elements revolve.

This is not always easily accomplished in driftwood designs since the strong individuality of the wood is thereby played against the strong "personality" of the figure. For instance, the magnificence of the driftwood in Plate 80 is overwhelming, yet the bird is the element that holds your attention. Because of its distinctive form and strong personality, as well as its placement, it is the special attraction. Take away the bird, and the design would be depleted. Another piece of material would have to be added to compensate, but a figure of lesser

138

Plate 83. A Chinese fisherman is an important element in this simple design of driftwood with three white ranunculus in a brass vase.

Plate 84. A heavy root section glued to a gently curving branch gives an effect of substance and airiness that seems right for this fruit and flower arrangement. The native figure duplicates the rhythmic lines of the wood. Color interest is developed by the gray of wood and base, the purple of grapes, and the chartreuse of seed pods, poplar blossoms and the Native's fruit basket.

Plate 85. Two broad green aspidistra leaves pull the arched ends of this gray driftwood down to earth where it is firmly held to its base with screws. Leafy twigs of pittosporum complete a setting for the bird figure.

Plate 86. Driftwood serves the dual role of container and linear structure for this arrangement of candytuft and loquat foliage. The white of the blossoms is repeated in the figure of the Japanese girl.

Plate 87. Red celosia is the red flag to this bull. The plumes of varicolored wheat and twists of vine increase the "taunting matador" effect, with the pocked driftwood already ripped by the menacing horns.

Plate 88. Two sections of wood have lines that relate to the form of the austere Chinese lady in this study in oriental mood. The wood framework is interrupted by sprigs of yellow-and-green euonymus and a castor-bean leaf. Yellow Fugi chrysanthemums make bright accents.

Plate 89. A strong wood form frames the featured figure, a Chinese gentleman. Both are brown. Artificial material—including chartreuse seed pods and pink-centered, green-petaled poplar blossoms—are used as a permanent arrangement.

Plate 90. Balanced pieces of tan-brown driftwood present a variety of strong lines, heightened by a dried philodendron pod of the same hue. Gray-green bryophyllum and a rich mahogany-colored bird add balance as well as textural and color interest.

interest could not compete with the dominance of the driftwood.

Omit the Chinese gentleman in Plate 25 and the design would not only lack a strong center of interest, it would also be thrown out of balance. The design in Plate 78 is aesthetically pleasing and harmonious, but it would not be complete without the bird, which continues the curve of line bringing it to a graceful ending. The figure featured as the center of interest in Plate 99 may be a little mite of a fellow but he certainly has personality plus. Try taking him out of the design and see what happens to its impact. Although the driftwood in Plate 100 is unusually strong, the form of the bird is so dynamic that it is unmistakably the star of the piece.

Figures can be the essence of dignity in a quiet background, increasing its depth (Plate 22), or they can be the perfect accent, dramatically expressive (Plate 77), or brilliantly beautiful (Plate 81).

Plate 98 reveals a couple of sneak thieves—a pair of gazelle figurines. It is obvious that the wondrously textured driftwood was intended to be the featured attraction. The photographer's superb lighting, however, has caught the feeling of the close of day, with the gazelles seeking the shelter and protection of the driftwood and castor-bean leaf for the night. I insist that these two figurines are thieves because they steal so much of the limelight here, when actually they were meant to be only an accent. But that's part of the game, too.

Dignity from Simplicity

Unity, dignity, simplicity—the three are interdependent. Remember, when you use figurines with driftwood, simplicity is the keynote. Only a minimum of plant material is necessary; at times none at all. Freedom from clutter in elements and details of construction spell simplicity, a quality not always easily achieved. One dramatic curve, as in Plate 95, proves the point.

8. Mood Pieces

Our moods, our emotions are usually somewhat mysterious even to ourselves. Driftwood offers an excellent means of expression. For an evocation of dark moods, look at Plates 91 and 92. For one of elation and excitement, consider Plate 93. Strong moods often seek expression in physical activity, and thus we turn to creative work for action that is effective yet offers a relaxation from tension.

One method of releasing tension is through artistic creation. Emotions of driving force require that we do something creatively new. When a situation presents a problem, it also offers an invitation to create. We need not be timid about trying new ways or expressing new ideas. These are always challenging.

Driftwood as an Aid

Driftwood offers a perfect means for depicting moods. Its vigor and versatility suggest to the artist many exciting mood-ideas. The unusual shapes present fascinating possibilities, suggestive to your imagination and provocative to your ingenuity. With perception of new forms and dimensions in the bold structure of driftwood, the arranger finds it easy to portray many moods.

They may be spiritual moods, expressing peace and harmony, as in Plate 94. With driftwood forming the shrine, we develop here an expression of love and adoration. Harmony prevails. Serenity is depicted in Plate 95; it seems to say: "Peace on earth, good will toward men."

Special lighting can aid in creating moods, increasing emotional intensity. In Plate 96, creative lighting adds impact to the design. The driftwood, painted white for harmony, frames the madonna and strengthens the ascending spiral in this somewhat modern interpretation.

In similar vein, the stillness of nature is stressed—the murmur of early morn or evening's closing vespers and solitude—as in Plates 97, 98, and 99.

Oriental in Feeling

Many driftwood pieces have an oriental aspect. Naturalism and linear simplicity are Japanese contributions to the art of flower arranging. Love of Nature and feeling for natural growth are expressed through the beauty of uncluttered lines. The arranger displays indi-

Plate 91. Four major objects offer four different textures: the torn, rough-hewn driftwood; the unfinished, chiseled, yet smoothly carved wooden figure; the tattered but substantial dried palm sprays, and the hard, shadow-softened surface of the stone base. All are in tones of brown and tan.

Plate 92. Without the mass of palm sprays, the driftwood used in Plate 91 emerges here with increased power. However, it does not establish any particular mood; it is dependent on accessories for that. The sense of weariness, perhaps hopelessness, of this composition flows from the wonderfully evocative figure of the monk, carved by the Mexican artist José Pinal. A few leafless twigs of the smoke tree lighten the somber effect.

Plate 93. In this interpretive study, dark, strong forms of drift-wood, representing the earth, establish the foundation for a silvery rocket with fruit to speak for the goodness of earth. The orange-red spirals (a decoration of shredded plastic on wire), shooting down from the rocket and out to the left and right, suggest the blast of a flaming ascent, the misty "angel hair," the typical blast-off cloud of smoke and steam.

Plate 94. In this mood piece, an effectively lighted, stately segment of driftwood serves as a shrine for the sandalwood figure of Ankara, the Javanese goddess of eternity and love, paying honor to a yellow daffodil. The sand-blasted wood reciprocates almost every line of the figure, and an old clump of agave makes an appropriate accent.

Plate 95. Inspirational lighting is the major factor here. Light streams down from Heaven to dramatize the figure of Madonna and Child. The emotional effect is increased by the lighting of only the upper half of the beautifully curved driftwood. Rubbed with gold tint, the figure harmonizes with the brown driftwood, the circular base, and the fabric table covering.

Plate 96. White-painted driftwood provides a frame and suggests the pattern for this arrangement. A spiral of wire, covered with glistening white shredded plastic, softens the background for the porcelain Madonna. Curled vines and skeletonized leaves balance the driftwood on the left, with pearlized grapes and flowers of white Formosan wood fibre on the right. The design is set on a block of white Carrara.

Plate 97. Crispness of a cold winter or early spring morning is expressed in this naturalistic study of two startled deer in a forest scene. A rhythmically grained, ladlelike piece of driftwood rests easily in a plow disc. Pine sprays lend essential softness.

Plate 98. With its fragment restored (at lower right), the drift-wood that seemed so vulnerable in Plate 87 is a tower of strength here. Like a decaying but still sturdy castle, it stands as a shelter for two gazelles. A light-silhouetted castor-bean leaf and chartreuse chrysanthemums are fitting accessories.

Plate 99. An emphatic silhouette is formed by two pieces of gray driftwood in a modern black container. Resting in sprays of juniper, high above the grassy gray earth, the gray owl suggests loneliness and solitude.

Plate 100. Two strong pieces of driftwood, bracing each other to form a free-standing unit, set the stage for a stylized, tragi-comic owl.

Plate 101. Two owl figures here share the limelight with a sturdy array of driftwood. By careful placement, three strong pieces are balanced on each other without mechanical aid. Green laurel leaves round out the base.

Plate 102. A picturesque, free-standing piece of wood and branches of laurel foliage, strong in oriental feeling, make an impressive design. The figure of an old Chinese rests securely on the sturdy perch. He makes a gay color accent of blue, green and beige against the brown and gray wood.

viduality by symbolizing a philosophical idea, accentuating a mood through a linear design.

This art is by no means new; in fact, it is many centuries old. Although we have adopted versions to fit our needs, much of it still suggests strong oriental influence. We may not arrange flowers symbolically, as the Japanese do, but we do seek simplicity of line and balanced harmony which are the basic requirements of beautiful design.

This inspiration, coming directly from Nature, results in interpretive designs revealing the close association between men and Nature. This affinity is stressed in the figurine-driftwood composition, Plate 102, in which an old man sits in meditation. Nature's grandeur is suggested in Plate 103; nostalgia envelopes the two old men as they near the end of life's span. And the dreamer, in a mood of whimsical fantasy, Plate 104, seeks the companionship and inspiration of Nature.

Driftwood Inspiration Moods

Those who love Nature in its many manifestations have found, or will find, that driftwood can inspire moods. Once you become aware of this, you will look for pieces that will help you create mood designs of distinction. In Plate 105, there is a mood of reminiscence—a

163

memory of sand and surf, pleasurable days of relaxation under blue skies and summer sun. The beauty of sea gulls in flight combines in our thoughts with the wonder of the boundless sea. The handsomely textured wood, found on a stroll along the seashore, inspired this piece. Others, as in Plates 106 and 109, bring back memories of happy vacation days.

An exalted mood, inspired by the grandeur of the strong forms of driftwood, is depicted in Plates 111 and 112. The animated figures of the horses emphasize the feeling. The addition of plant material is unnecessary. Driftwood mood pieces are, indeed, interesting to work out, and offer a great opportunity for creativity.

Plate 103. Two glue-joined sections of wood, one a long low arch and the other a powerful vertical thrust, create a memorable setting for a pair of Chinese figures. The impact of the picture is due to the balance of scale between figures and driftwood. The introduction of flowers, foliage or other plant material would destroy the strength of the effect. I call this one "Life's Span."

Plate 104. In this composition of battered brown wood, green laurel and bristly, burned palms, the day-dreaming woodcarver figure steals the scene. A slate blue coat increases his dominance.

Plate 105. Gouged and riddled like the coral reefs along the shore where it was found, this piece of driftwood is a study in itself. With the addition of coral and realistic sea gulls, it epitomizes ocean shores everywhere.

Plate 106. Slightly altered, accented only by coral and a branch of dried sea grape and set at a different angle, the coral-like wood of Plate 105 is seen here in a new aspect, but still in a magic-of-the-sea arrangement.

Plate 107. A silvery cypress root of smooth texture makes a frame for this mood piece of the sea. Waves and a breeze are suggested by the line direction of the root tips and dried brown seaweed. Shells and coral add contrast of texture and variety of form.

Plate 108. The same strong, marvelously textured piece, as in
Plate 98 and others, here holds aloft a writhing spray of seed
pods from a palm tree. The pod stem is joined to the wood with
floral clay; tufts of lichen hide the mechanics; lumps of fungi add
earthiness. Values of tan and brown pervade the free-standing
design which I call "Driftwood Rhythm."

Plate 109. Found on the beach at Hilton Head Island, South Carolina, this patterned wood with its foundation of fungus slabs, would be the main interest in any design. The fungus, the wood, the spray of dried broom and the curly-leaved, dried plants (found growing on the sand dunes), all offer softly blending hues of brown.

Plate 110. Harsh lines and texture of this free-standing gray driftwood are set off by the smooth black birds, green, thread-specked shafts of yucca and two clipped palmetto leaves. All the parts stand out boldly against the bright light. Not a restful design, it nevertheless is completely natural.

Plate 111. Braced with smaller pieces for balance, this magnificent driftwood specimen—full of wild grandeur—forms a setting
for the lithe figures of young horses. The untamed vitality of
the design needs no plant material or other accessories. The rich
brown of the horses enlivens the gray wood.

Plate 112. This unbelievable piece of natural sculptured drift-wood with its textural quality, twirls and twists is a thoroughly satisfying art piece by itself. The stallion (dark brown, with white mane and tail) brings to the picture a highly dramatic feeling. The driftwood's inherent fascination is such that different figures, or a different placement of the wood (see Plate 77) may be used to create other moods.

Plate 113. A strong, rhythmically curved piece of driftwood sets the pattern for this Thanksgiving study. Accessories enlarge the scheme. The brown of turkey and driftwood, the rosy-lavender of the zinnias and the green-orange of the acorn squash are echoed in the pendulous berried branches; the pokeberries are green at the tips, graduating from light to dark purple.

Plate 114. Painted white and set in a block of Styrofoam, driftwood frames an original yet traditional Christmas design.
Trimmed, whitened palmetto, flocked thistle pods, chartreuse
Christmas balls with sprays of artificial material and a white
reindeer figurine contribute to the picture. All stems have been
inserted into the Styrofoam, eliminating the need for a needlepoint. The coral pink of the pods and sprays adds a modern
touch.

9. For the Flower Show

Current trends in creative flower arranging have all but obliterated the old-time basket plumped full of a lovely conglomeration of flowers from the garden. Flowers alone used to be enough to inspire even the non-artistic person to try a hand at arranging. Through the years, growing methods have improved and hybridizers have developed new colors and more perfect forms. But more than floral beauty is needed to compete with the high creativity found in flower-show work today, where almost anything—with or without flowers—can be used to interpret themes.

Public Expectations

At show time, with the judging all finished, the last ribbon placed, doors opened to welcome visitors, you heave a sigh of relief. Excitement and pride in a job well done keep you from feeling the weariness of long hours spent working on the show. As you listen to comments of visitors, you naturally edge nearer to your own exhibit to catch what is being said about it. If you listen on the sidelines long enough, you will find out exactly what you should have done but didn't do, and also what never should have been done in the first place. You will hear your arrangement unmercifully criticized and torn apart. About the time you are thinking of retreating through the nearest door, you hear the pleasant sound of "ah's" and "oh's" coming from the next group of viewers in front of your niche. *They* think the whole thing is a work of artful beauty!

Never underestimate the opinions of your flower-show public. Many of them are expert arrangers themselves, even flower-show judges, and know good design when they see it. Their criticisms are worth listening to. The majority of the visitors are well informed on the subject of originality and distinction, and have an excellent conception of both qualities. They are seeking the inspiration and aesthetic pleasure that come with viewing creative arranging. They are looking for something above the average, something different. It is up to you to see that they are not disappointed but will find what they seek, at least in your own design.

After the show is over and you have had time to assimilate the remarks overheard, take inventory and resolve to bring keener imaginative planning, a more individual approach and a renewal of courage to your work. In my experience, I have found three things to be most pertinent to the art of flower arranging, and especially to driftwood arranging. They are creative imagination, courage and freedom of expression.

Creative Imagination

The crystal-like beauty of a newly opened rose bathed in early morning dew can inspire a song; a lovely countryside at sunset can suggest a sonnet. The creative work of others, a painting, a poem, a piece of sculpture, can fill the mind with the glow of inspiration and imagination. There are many sources of inspiration and each is a virtual storehouse of ideas. But nature with an infinite beauty of forms, color and textures is one of the greatest sources.

Inspiration is the spark that kindles the imagination, and imagination is at the heart of all creative talent. Each time a new form of art has emerged, a new style of architecture has appeared or even a change in trends in our own world of flower arranging has occurred, someone with creative imagination has had the courage to act on his beliefs.

Creative imagination is for the bold of heart and mind who are unafraid to venture, unafraid to do the

179

new, no matter how shocking it may seem; it is for those who have a free scope to experiment and a desire to contribute something of lasting value. Above all, these creators have the courage to act on their convictions. They are the ones who are projecting exciting new concepts of creativeness and contributing to the advancement of art. Your imagination can prove your individuality, and it is individuality, not conformity, that leads to originality and distinction.

Creative Courage

Do we have the courage to be different, the courage to soar above the subjectivism of so-called rules, or do we complacently ride along with the tide of conformity, which ultimately results in mediocrity?

Courage—that most admirable virtue of human nature—must be possessed by the arranger who aspires to creativeness. You must have the courage to be bold, to dare, to break with convention—not for the sake of eccentricity, but because of an inner compulsion for self-expression.

Formulated ways of thinking are not acceptable to the artist whose creative impulses urgently demand recognition. He isn't willing to follow the herd in its stampede to conformity, but has an unflagging desire to

be different, a capacity for imaginative and original outlook. He has the ability to think for himself and the
courage to speak out for his convictions and to act upon
them.

It is easy to let someone else do the exploring and be
the pioneer. It is comfortable to follow along when the
pattern has been set. But new ideas have largely been
discovered by the individual thinker and doer who has
the initial courage to pursue outward expressions in artistic interpretations.

Flower-show themes offer challenging opportunities
for creative courage. Provocative class titles serve as
springboards to inspiration, inflaming the imagination
and stimulating the urge to create. New ideas and freshness of approach can result in striking designs and give
to your arrangement that quality which will stop the
crowds at your exhibit—if you have creative courage!

Freedom of Expression

Self-expression is one of the prime purposes of working in any art. One of the requirements for a good
flower arrangement, if it is to be original and distinctive, is complete freedom of expression based on sound
fundamentals. The creative thinker must not be stifled
by sets of rules which serve no purpose but to lessen his

self-confidence in his ability, sapping his self-reliance and his individual daring and initiative. A high degree of awareness and a keen sensitivity to the surrounding world give the artist more insight and understanding, resulting in a freshness of outlook that wipes clear the vision dimmed by acceptance of conformity.

Conformity in art is no virtue, and the passive acceptance of someone else's standards does not develop our own taste. Neither our aesthetic nor artistic desires can be fulfilled unless we express our own imaginative and original ideas. With freedom of thought and expression, we can endow our designs with a spiritual dimension that is found in all worth-while art. Driftwood is one of the countless media nature offers the artist who seeks a creative outlet. Its intrinsic beauty of line and sculptural forms offer challenging possibilities.

Interpretive Designs

The interpretive and artistic use of driftwood in flower arranging increases in popularity year by year. Flower shows now regularly offer classes for it. Each year my club has a section of the show for driftwood, a feature our visitors have come to look forward to. Proof of the impressiveness of this section, even to the younger set, are the comments of a small boy visiting one of the

182

shows with his mother. When they reached the drift-wood classes, he was heard to say: "Mother, just look what they have done with those old rotten limbs!" Evidently he wasn't the only one impressed. The judges were, too. The top award was given to the composition in Plate 115 whose textural quality may well have given it the appearance of being rotten. The class title was, "Along the Trail," and what could be more natural than this woodsy scene?

Plate 116 interprets the theme of "Twilight in the Garden." There is a peaceful atmosphere as the twilight hour comes to the garden. Hushed quietness and restful anticipation are felt as the shadows creep in, and the towering driftwood assures protection to the egret for the coming night.

The strong oriental feeling of the driftwood in Plate 117 inspired and set the pattern of the theme of "In the Oriental Manner." The old Chinese man was inspirational, too, and aided in carrying out the theme. The fish basket on his back suggested his activity, thus the fishnet was displayed in the background to emphasize the suggestion. Cattail foliage and a water-lily on a stone base complete the design. There is good relationship between all elements here; each relates in some way to water, and the whole is strongly oriental.

Many of the interpretations in this book are ideas inspired by the driftwood itself rather than by a flower-show theme. For instance, the composition in Plate 118 was inspired by the structure of the wood form which suggested the thought of an empty tomb. I call it "Easter Morn." Easter lilies were not in season when I first felt the urge to create this piece, but what a joy it was to work out the idea when they did arrive. The story of the crucifixion and resurrection are told simultaneously by the cross, stones and the empty tomb—symbolically interpretive of the greatest miracle of all time. The ethereal light surrounding the "tomb" and the whiteness of the lilies signify the purity of a risen Christ.

The same piece of driftwood, proving its versatility, is used in a reversed position for the design in Plate 119, which I call "The Garden of Eden." The obvious interpretation is Eve being tempted by the serpent to eat

Plate 115. The final fourteen illustrations presented here (Plates 115 through 127) illustrate interpretive flower-show themes.
ALONG THE TRAIL. This twisted, weather-gouged piece of wood is appropriate to the title of this study. The rough pine-slab base blends harmoniously in color and texture. Sprigs of pine lighten the outline. Small white chrysanthemums represent daisies growing along the trail. The white bear figurine adds a sense of movement.

Plate 116. TWILIGHT IN THE GARDEN. Secured on the base with screws, the strong wood form used in Plate 85 is employed with equal impact here. A dramatic setting for a snowy egret is enhanced by lighting that suggests the twilight hour. Spikey stems of water grass, curlicues of staghorn fern, and a bristly formation of coral make a setting for the porcelain figurine.

Plate 117. IN THE ORIENTAL MANNER. A Chinese fisherman, carved of dark red teakwood, seems to admire the beauty
of a pink lotus blossom, growing at the foot of a spiraling branch,
a free-standing piece set on a stone base. The brown fishnet
dangling down out of the darkness suggests the hulking side
of a ship. Vertical lines of cattail foliage offer contrast to the
pattern of the net and the curved line of the brown driftwood.

Plate 118. EASTER MORN. "And the third day He arose again from the dead"—the words fit the picture; the great stone, rolled away from the mouth of the cave, reveals the empty tomb. The unusual formation of this driftwood suggested a dramatic Easter scene. The cross in the dark background and the glistening lilies are integral parts of any portrayal of this universal theme.

Plate 119. GARDEN OF EDEN. In a reversed position, the same piece of wood used for Easter Morn (Plate 118) supplies the framework for this interpretation. Tempted by the serpent (the twisted poinciana bean pod), Eve seems about to eat the fruit from the tree of knowledge (represented by the small palm-tree branch in the background). Such an exquisite frame of driftwood can contribute to many different constructions.

Plate 120. ARRANGEMENT COMPLEMENTING A MOD-ERN PAINTING. This painting of the design in Plate 119, "The Garden of Eden," is by photographer Leonid Skvirsky. To form the framework for the complementing arrangement, two sections of wood were secured with screws. Castor-bean stalks and foliage arranged with strelitzia surround the "Spirit of Love," represented by the figure of Ankara (Plate 94) here depicted as interceding for Eve. Since the painting was executed especially for this design, the colors were correlated. The blue background of the painting is picked up by blue in the strelitzias, the orange, re-peated in the empty seed pod at the foot of Eve in the painting. The rich brown of the poinciana pod picks up the color of the tall castor-bean stalks in the arrangement. More castor-bean leaves round off the base. The frame of the painting was antiqued to blend with the driftwood in the arrangement.

Plate 121. LIFE AND DEATH. Strongly curved driftwood furnishes line interest and gives balance to this dramatic presentation. The hope of eternal life is represented by the lone flower growing from the eye-socket of the bleached skull.

the fruit of the forbidden tree, seen in the background. This composition, bordering on surrealism, could not be called a floral arrangement by any standards, but nevertheless it is a free interpretive expression—maybe bold, but essentially creative.

An amalgam of two art forms is shown in Plate 120. The oil painting based on the composition of "The Garden of Eden" is by Leonid Skvirsky, who photographed all the designs for this book. This idea was conceived when I was asked to do a modern arrangement complementing a modern painting. The interpretation here is the Spirit of Love interceding for Eve as she is about to take the fateful step that will reveal to her the evils of the world.

As in all modern art, everyone will not sympathize with this style, nor indeed any style that does not particularly appeal to individual taste. But since art is not a restricted province, we must recognize the right of each person to create that which expresses his personal taste, and to interpret his thoughts and ideas with freedom.

Almost anything other than flowers may be used in interpretive designing. Plate 121 shows a portrayal of "Life and Death," a provocative theme for a flower show. With a title such as this, the imagination works

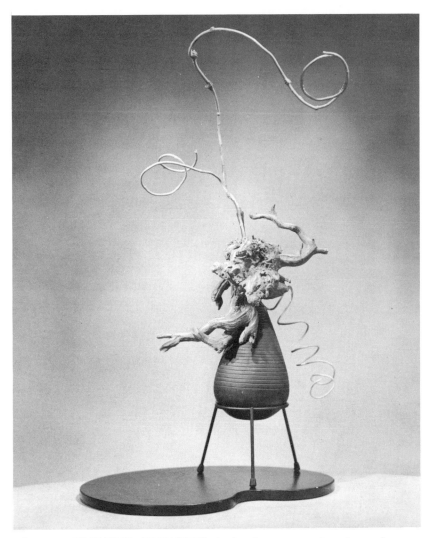

Plate 122. FLIGHTS OF FANCY. A chunky root section (waxed to bring out the brown hue) forms the center of interest in this modern design. Beige-colored honeysuckle vines have been peeled, curled and dried to form the flighty lines. The polished base and the tapered container give balance and add to the modern feeling.

Plate 123. TROPICAL SPLENDOR. A powerfully proportioned piece of wood furnishes the main interest for this equatorial theme. (Driftwood like this would dominate any design.) Dried palm branches and clumps of coral complement the wood's sculptural beauty by repeating its deep serrations. A small piece of wood is screwed to the back to make the piece free-standing.

Plate 124. MARCH WINDS. Laurel roots, streaming in the wind, create a sense of motion and form the linear structure for this interpretation. Tattered edges and points of dried artichokes give needed substance. Added body and color accent are provided by white, curled-edged leaves from the cecropia (snakewood) tree.

Plate 125. SPRING ROMANCE. Rhythmic driftwood, mounted on the base with screws, furnishes a pleasing line for this interpretation. Leafy mountain laurel branches with pink blossoms set a spring mood for the birds.

Plate 126. GRECIAN CULTURE. Fresh green, spiky, unfurled leaves from the heart of a century plant are the "strings" of the Grecian "lyre" formed by the curving, gray-toned driftwood. Gray-green echeveria links them together and contributes to the strong contrast of lines, shapes and colors.

Plate 127. ELEGANT SIMPLICITY. A storm-wracked yet still substantial bough is accented by the simple dignity of the succulent. The soft, subdued gray-green of the plant is also in harmony with the brown tones of the wood.

to the limit. With no schedule restrictions as to materials used, creativity had free rein. How could the interpretation best be worked out—something subtle or something startling? A subtle interpretation will leave much to the imagination and so be stimulating to a viewer, but often a less imaginative mind fails to grasp the intended meaning. On the other hand, the realistic, unexpected, even shocking interpretation presents its message strongly, leaving no room for vague wondering.

As thoughts and ideas swirl through the head of the designer who is planning such a bold interpretation, little misgivings begin to gnaw at the mind. Is the interpretation too bold and stark? The obvious, of course, could be done. A subtle, stylized design could be worked out, using appropriate plant material, but the total effect probably would be without much feeling. New ideas are always challenging, so why be timid? Why not have the courage to freely express this strong emotion? Imagination without courage to express it is not worth much.

What could have more impact than a realistic portrayal of the theme, with creative lighting employed to increase the effectiveness—dark shadows emphazing the mystery surrounding its bleakness? Perhaps the skull is a gruesome interpretation, but then what is more gruesome than death? What is more awe-inspiring than the incomprehensibleness of death? Although we may struggle despairingly with physical death, we hold fast to the hope of life eternal. The lone, struggling flower, springing from the eye-socket of the skull, brings to us this message, and the reassurance of hope and ultimate victory of life.

Highly emotional themes, such as this one, probably are not found too often in flower shows. However, should you find that you are to interpret a theme stressing emotions—or if you simply wish to do so for your own enjoyment—do not be afraid to portray your impressions, for it is here that your individuality comes to the fore.

Interpretive designing with driftwood is fun; there's no limit to the range of interesting interpretations that can be worked out. So let *your* imagination add pleasure to your life—with the artistic use of driftwood.

Part III
TOWARD THE ABSTRACT

10. New Designs with Wood

Driftwood with its wondrous shapes and rhythmic structure has inspired many imaginative designs. As arrangers have developed a bold, provocative approach to their work and learned to handle space, form and color in freer ways, they have reflected the challenge of the times and produced arresting designs of contemporary expression. Imagination is virtually the only limit to creativity. New and unusual materials, combined with unique formations of driftwood, lead to a new world of driftwood designing.

New experiences make us aware that new evaluations and decisions must be made if we are to reflect the trends of the times. Stereotyped styles have become outmoded because they are not directly concerned with the world today, and we find we cannot leave flower arrangement to tradition alone. Even though we continue to enjoy certain aspects of the past, we need to give thought to the world we now live in. By experimenting and broadening our point of view, we can create designs expressive of *our* way of life.

Recent Trends

One of the trends we are aware of today, and one to which driftwood lends itself beautifully, is abstraction. Although abstraction is as old as art itself, direct consideration of it is fairly new to flower arrangers. To many, abstract designs are strange and uncomfortable—if not distasteful—perhaps the result of not being able to approach them with an open mind, and of searching instead for established patterns. We tend to dislike the unfamiliar and find it hard to interpret—as in much of modern art.

Of the three general categories of realism, expressionism and abstraction, apparently the least understood is abstraction, even though it is basic to all art. Realism, as applied to flower arrangement, often results in an easily perceived scene from nature with materials placed naturally and without distortion. In Plates 23, 29, 44, 48, for example, driftwood suggests a tree or branch associated with growing flowers. Expressionist pieces tend to be interpretative (Plates 55, 59, 65, 66), less literal, with materials often placed in somewhat unnatural positions

204

or in unnatural associations, but there is always little doubt as to what they actually are.

Analysis of Abstraction

Abstract designs may seem radical on first viewing, and may be rejected as new concepts often are, but is it not unintelligent to reject forms of art that are new or unconventional simply because they are not familiar? Of course we cannot like everything produced by contemporary artists, but we *can try* to understand their work. There are many ways of expressing an idea, and abstract flower arranging is one of them. It is a new, stimulating challenge, and it is essentially creative.

When we analyze an abstract design, we are immediately aware of several aspects. We find that it does not make a concrete statement in the way a little scene does; rather it makes a more general statement. It suggests and implies (Plate 135), but leaves specific interpretation to the viewer. A completely abstract arrangement does not depict a recognizable environment or object; it is wholly nonrepresentational. Materials may be reshaped, massed or distorted until they lose their identity (Plate 151); they are used nonrealistically for the designer's own purpose. In fact, we might say that abstract design is an expression in line, form, color, texture and space, with no resemblance to nature.

Since abstraction generalizes, it can be symbolic; it encompasses many meanings. The designer may be expressing an idea or interpreting a personal experience in a way not immediately accessible to another (Plate 145). An abstract design may or may not be "pretty"; it is always open to interpretation. As a projection of your subjective world what results may be an expression that pleases your fancy or aesthetic sense, a design not concerned with a portrayal of nature, a handling of materials to suit your own purpose.

There are degrees of abstraction: distortion may be slight or extensive. As the materials in a design lose their original identity and take on new aspects, the degree of abstraction increases. It is almost impossible to achieve pure abstraction in flower arranging since natural materials can hardly be distorted so far that they are unrecognizable. Consequently, abstract flower arrangements fall somewhere between realism and total abstraction. They are likely to be interpretive or decorative abstractions in which the design itself becomes the subject.

The New Freedom

In considering abstract designs we bring our own experiences and perceive what we are accustomed to see

206

and feel. Our imagination goes beyond the immediate subject and works with the artist's concept. Thus our insight combines with the artist's expression—and both interpret. There may be as many interpretations of an abstract design as there are those who view it. However, there need be no "translation" or interpretation, but simply an experience of plastic elements in a composition—a pleasing interrelationship of line, form, space, color and texture.

Liberation from past restrictions has given us freedom to handle materials in our own way, to experiment. Abstraction has produced an art from which we will do well to ponder, and with which we should become familiar. Today it may seem like nonsense, but tomorrow it may well be truth.

207

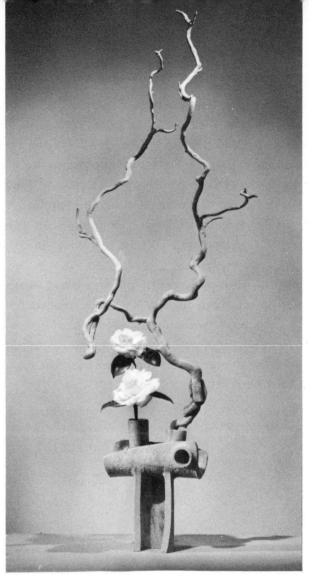

Plate 128. This rhythmical piece of driftwood gracefully twists into space, arching at the left over two blush-pink camellias, and rising vertically to form two branches. Both the wood and the soft tan ceramic, so much a part of the design, were rubbed lightly with pink chalk to blend them with the delicate hue of the flowers. In this design of modern feeling, space and shallow planes—established by the two necks of the ceramic—are dominant.

Plate 129. A magnificent driftwood form swirls from one of the small openings of the tan ceramic. Two pink roses with foliage and a large philodendron leaf thrust upward to give necessary height to this semi-abstract design.

Plate 130. Like a bowknot of ribbon, this twisted branch is as intricate in shape as the strelitzia flower that emerges like a phoenix for ascension. Following the line of the bootlike container, with loops enclosing spaces that counterbalance height, the branch terminates in another enclosure. The natural distortion of the wood intensifies the abstraction.

Plate 131. Creating a different atmosphere, the branch used in Plate 130 proves its versatility. Although placed differently, the line again compliments that of the container. Two pointed strelitzias provide contrast of form and a colorful accent for the tan branch and ceramic; the flowers also contribute force to an already dynamic semi-abstract design.

Plate 132. In this semi-abstraction, long curved branches of a large piece of gray driftwood give horizontal emphasis and sinuous movement up and around the yucca stalk, creating depth and enclosing free-form areas of space. Firmly anchored in a stack of concrete blocks, the yucca provides a strong vertical element with terminal spikes. Textural interest is increased by distortion of the foliage, which has been clipped in varying blunted lengths.

Plate 133. Integrating with space and serving as a support for the stemless flowers, this tall, two-pronged piece of driftwood echoes the shape of the container. Three white chrysanthemum heads, suspended by invisible nylon fishing cord, twirl in space like snowflakes. One philodendron leaf completes this near abstraction.

Plate 134. Two sections of driftwood, fastened with screws, are balanced securely on the sculpture-container along with brush-like African seed pods and flat serrated leaves. Stark lighting and a monochromatic scheme of dull browns in pods, wood and ceramic, contribute to the interpretation of a winged scavenger momentarily alighting to investigate the seed-pod offering. These same sections of wood, used in Plate 80 in a contemporary design as part of a setting for a carved bird, take on quite different connotations in this abstraction.

Plate 135. This near-abstract composition could be viewed simply as a design, but it was made to represent the controversial wheat transaction between the United States and Russia, which took place some time ago. The scythe that is a symbol of Russia, the bundle of wheat and the broken stems of the orange-red seed pods like broken promises tell the story. A heavy piece of machinery appropriately supports the design.

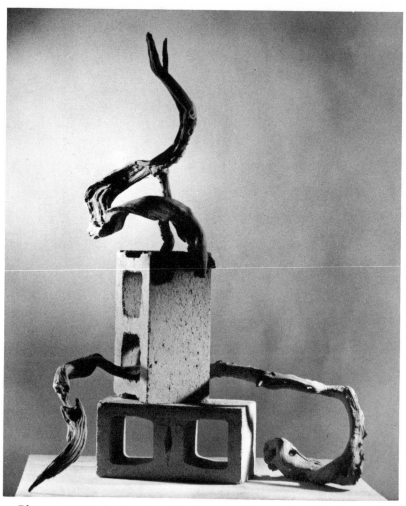

Plate 136. Two concrete blocks provide stand and container for strong driftwood forms in an abstract design open to interpretation. A feeling of depth is developed by passing one section of wood through the hole in the diagonally placed block, by the front to back movement of the wood and by the square spaces enclosed by wood and blocks. Dramatic lighting is important in this composition that emphasizes form, texture and space.

Plate 137. By adding an abstracted branch of spiky palm and changing the lighting, the design in Plate 136 takes on different implications. There is a new emphasis on texture, the branch jutting diagonally divides the free open space on the right into two sections, thus increasing the complexity of the design.

Plate 138. Two sections of driftwood and rounded sea fans, sharply silhouetted, make a grotesque setting for this weird dried object from the sea that could be a creature from Davy Jones' locker, its tail looped to its back, gleefully swinging its feet over a sea of coarse white pebbles. The lighting suggests moonlight and mystery while enhancing the texture of the sea fans and the strong rhythms of the wood.

Plate 139. Supported in a Japanese bowl on a carved stand, this strong piece of driftwood develops a rhythmical line as it moves down from the left through two white chyrsanthemums and a spray of glossy camellia foliage up into free space. With materials fully recognizable, and bowl, stand and base used in customary fashion, this design is slightly abstracted through the position of the wood, and placement of the mums.

Plate 140. The gay mood set by the black-and-white decoration and flare of the ceramic is continued by the black length of wood which frames two white calla lilies as it twirls out into space. This is a semi-abstract design with a feeling of light-hearted merriment.

Plate 141. This is a contemporary table setting with an Oriental influence. The black-satin finish of the angled wood matches the hand-rubbed teakwood stand, and relates as well to the soft sheen of the placemats. Gleaming white china complements the white tulips and variegated hosta foliage. In Plate 140 this piece of wood is used to convey a different feeling in a more abstracted design.

Plate 142. Two sections of wood (both used in Plate 138) are fastened together to form a figure eight. A section of sewer pipe serves as container and white pebbles as base for an X-shaped arrangement of bright red anthuriums and large dark oval leaves. This composition can be viewed simply as a compact vertical design with two loops of wood encompassing space, or interpreted in timely fashion as a space capsule with astronauts —a topic I had in mind when I made the arrangement.

Plate 143. Strong diagonal movement in the driftwood section determined the patterns of this design. The straight-sided cylinder in muted earthy colors gives vertical movement, continued by the taller stem, while diagonal movement is repeated in the coral anthuriums and their leaves. These also create a strong area of interest. Space delineated by the stems and pointed buds counterbalances the weight and activity below.

11. With Wood, Wire, Plastic and Glass

New materials have been introduced into contemporary flower arrangement that would have been unacceptable a few years ago. Glass, plastic, wire and metal, even scrap from the junkyard, are now used in bold, original designs. In fact any material that interests the flower arranger turns up in designs today. And, happily, driftwood can be combined with most materials to make even more distinctive designs.

New Materials

Wire is one of the newer materials I have found particularly interesting and stimulating to work with, especially in combination with driftwood. It is similar to the woody vines of honeysuckle, grape and wisteria, and functions in a composition in much the same way—notably as lines in space. Wire also presents textural variation. Because of its flexibility it is an asset in delineating space and, with a little effort, wire can be bent into almost any shape. However, you do need to develop patience and skill in handling wire. Once bent in one direction, it is not easily reversed without leaving undesirable kinks which cannot be straightened. It is best to have your pattern in mind first, then carefully twist the wire to conform. You may need to use pliers, especially if the wire is large and not easily shaped.

In the designs in this chapter you will note that various forms of wire have been used. The tinsel-like material hanging from the center of the arrangement in Plate 146 is from wire-weaving looms. At times, after wire is woven, the edges are trimmed, and these trimmings curl into tight little ringlets that provide interesting textures and forms. If the wire is from aluminum screening it is likely to be available in many colors. But you can get any color you want with a spray-on paint (Plate 156). Another type of metal useful for the frame of a design is aluminum rod (Plate 151). And thin, pliable wire has been used in Plate 147 and painted a pale pink.

In keeping with the modern pursuit of exploring the junkyard, I have transformed a plow disc (Plate 148), a sprinkler guard (Plate 152) and a car spring (Plate 154) into containers. And in Plate 153, shaped metal scraps from a Venetian-blind factory are the basis of the design.

Other materials from industrial sources such as glass and plastic can also be used. Plastic strips and rod are combined in Plate 155 with glass discs, and in Plate 157 glass discs are again used but with a vine instead of synthetic material. It is only one step further to come full circle and use slender pieces of woody growth as wire, which is what I have done in Plate 158.

Plate 144. Decorative wrought iron makes a symmetrical frame
for trimmed apple-green palmettos, gray wood and curls of
bright red grass, moistened and wrapped with wire for shaping.
This is a colorful design with clearly defined spaces, curling
lines and pleated fan-shaped planes.

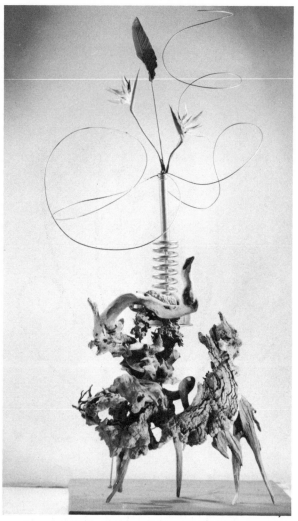

Plate 145. A surrealistic fantasy to be variously interpreted, this eleven-foot construction is made of a weathered stump (sculptured by nature), a car spring, loops of wire and two strelitzia flowers and a leaf that look, in this context, like pieces of metal. At the center, partially concealed, is an electric turntable that allows the upper half of the composition to revolve slowly. Thus actual motion is combined with motion implied by the lines and intricate rhythms of the wood. A tall stand supports the wire construction.

Plate 146. Screwed to a board and set firmly in a box of white pebbles, a length of driftwood holds a looped wire abstraction. At the left the curved horn of the wood establishes a rhythm which is continued by loops of wire that outline free-form spaces. Shiny strands of curled aluminum hang in a cluster of different texture, while clipped palmettos, painted orange-red, make bright accents for this airy composition. The substantial base of black wood encloses a volumetric space and supports the nine-foot construction. Ends of the wire were taped together and inserted in holes drilled in the wood.

Plate 147. Wire, wood and flowers are combined in this semi-abstraction. Forming the line of interest, rhythmical driftwood winds into two prongs, offsetting the weight below. Slender lines of the wood suggested the use of looped wires, painted to blend with the rosy hue of the camellias. The modern ceramic is soft green.

Plate 148. Black-painted driftwood fingers point toward a branch of clipped, dried palm, curved and trimmed while fresh. A spiral of peeled honeysuckle vine repeats in open shape the rounds of white flowers made from Formosan wood fiber, their delicacy in pleasant contrast to the stark abstracted elements. A plow disc, set on a metal tripod, adds to the modern aspect of this semi-abstract design.

Plate 149. Deliberate isolation of driftwood sections and dried palmettos allows each to be clearly seen and places emphasis on form and space in this abstraction. Plant material has been organized with contribution to design the primary consideration —and without regard for its natural qualities. Textural variations in white petals, tan-gray wood and soft brown palmettos are evident in contrast to the smooth cylinders of the olive-green container and the quietness of spaces. The eye moves easily through this open design where, as in many abstractions, no single element dominates.

Plate 150. Like a flash of lightning, this root formation zigzags
with terrific force from one of the triangular openings in the
ridged ceramic that here is inverted. Two daffodils reiterate
the diagonal which directs attention upward to the strong
horizontal. This abstraction is basically a design of lines and
spaces on a single shallow plane, with volume enclosed in the
container. Geometry predominates.

Plate 151. For a class assignment, "Transportation," plant material has been used abstractly and combined with wire to suggest a specific object, a helicopter. A framework of aluminum rods supports clipped, inverted palm sheaths (the split sections grow next to the trunk). These are inserted into hollow textile shuttles anchored to the projecting ends of the rods. A sea-sponge basket holding a cluster of scrap iron suggests cargo, and the dried papyrus plants, the propeller.

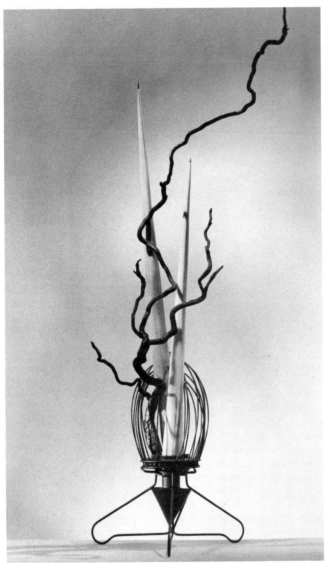

Plate 152. Serving as a launching pad for two abstract missiles—
spikes of the century plant—is an old sprinkler guard from
a junkyard, placed on a three-legged Christmas-tree stand. Black
driftwood, in dynamic upward movement, like black smoke from
an explosion, forms the main rhythmic line of the arrangement.

Plate 153. White scraps of metal from a Venetian-blind factory are the basis of this design made with soft green, almost white, spikes of yucca. The spiralling base and thrusting diagonals give to this geometric assemblage action and force. Serrated edges contrast with sharp points and clearly outlined spaces. Lighting creates effective shadows and a sense of depth.

Plate 154. This arrangement, poised on a tripod, derives its vitality from pronounced imbalance being brought into balance. A black car spring, welded at an acute angle to the tripod, presents a challenge which is met by an equally dynamic diagonal of two sections of driftwood. The wood also delineates an oblong of space which provides an airy enclosure for the plant material. Stems of monstera leaves and the foliage itself continue diagonal movement. Each piece is one in a series of checks and balances. The wood has been rubbed pale green to blend with the green leaves. In lively contrast are two red dahlias.

Plate 155. White orchids enclosed in transparent boxes made from clear plastic strips are given vertical placement. Around them encircling plastic rods seem to be in motion. A base of green-glass discs and wood blocks contributes to the round-and-round action. Stems and needleholders are wrapped with green floral tape to carry color up through the composition; bits of yucca bring green to the top. By surrounding the fragile orchids with a geometrical construction, a sense of imprisonment is conveyed—perhaps of caged fluttering birds. Rods are anchored to pinholders by taping short lengths of wire to the ends of the rods and pressing these into the holders. Yucca conceals the holder that contains the rods, and tape hides orchid tubes.

Plate 156. With head reverently bowed, a Madonna stands amid glistening glitter-treated foliage and shining satin balls on a Styrofoam pedestal. Her halo is made of wire painted white and freely looped. By its dimension and lofty position, it gives a modern touch to an ancient theme. Lighting increases the ethereal atmosphere of this all-white design.

Plate 157. Two translucent green-glass circles establish tranquil rounds that set the mood for this design. Verticals of stem and branch, subdued by placement behind the glass, still provide linear structure, while curving honeysuckle vine in clear silhouette gives rhythm and dimension. The tall green leaf is placed in a space that repeats the pointed shape of the leaf, and the shape of the pink anthurium is echoed by a loop at the far right. The free form, outlined by the vine on the left, reinterprets the discs. This semi-abstract of line, form, space, light and shadow suggests a moonlight scene.

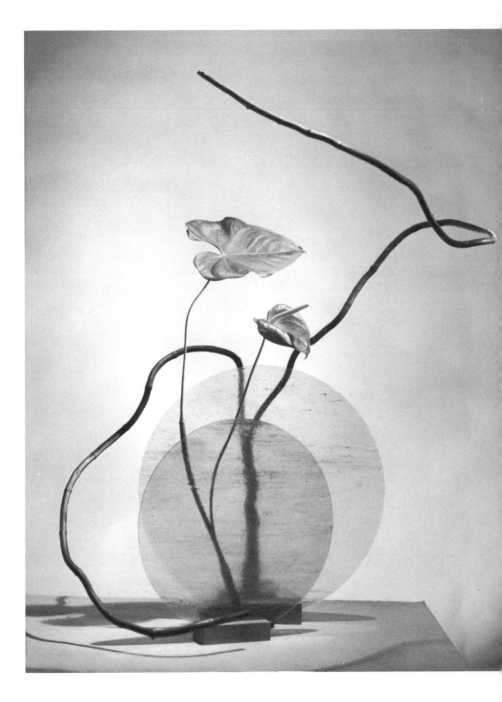

Plate 158. Slender vines, twisted in natural growth, look like wire bent into angles and curves. The sculptured wood, rubbed with chalk of various colors, blends with the reddish-brown of the padre figure quietly meditating in the garden. Green laurel foliage and yellow daffodils complement the brown tones of the other materials and complete a serene abstraction.

Plate 159. Line, form, color, texture and space are emphasized in this near-abstract design of crooked-neck gourds, a palm spathe, dahlia flower and philodendron leaf. These are seen primarily as design elements rather than as plant materials. The ceramic, important for its form and texture, serves as support for the curved lines that enclose spaces similar to the shape of the gourds. The vertical spathe contributes height and thrust in opposition to the forms below. Texture and color of green leaf and orange dahlia contrast with the smooth soft tans of other materials and are also balancing factors.

Plate 160. Circles of white plastic as well as lighting call attention to the white chrysanthemum perched on an intricate weathered upright of driftwood, as do the directional lines of plastic leading to it. A section of pipe provides a simple cylindrical support, its smooth form interrupted by two additional chrysanthemums. Angles of wood, circles of flowers and plastic—and the spaces made by both—are displayed in the modern idiom.

Index

Numbers in *italic* refer to illustrations

245

INDEX

247